The SCOPE OF MUSIC

By PERCY CARTER BUCK

Essay Index Reprint Series

BOOKS FOR LIBRARIES PRESS
FREEPORT, NEW YORK

First Published 1924
Reprinted 1969

STANDARD BOOK NUMBER:
8369-1276-4

LIBRARY OF CONGRESS CATALOG CARD NUMBER:
70-93321

PRINTED IN THE UNITED STATES OF AMERICA

*In our flesh grows the branch of this life,
in our soul it bears fruit.*

BROWNING : *Saul.*

CONTENTS

PREFACE

In the spring of 1923 I was invited to become 'Cramb Lecturer' in Glasgow University. The duties consisted in delivering ten lectures which dealt with some aspect of the Art of Music. As I had the honour of being the first lecturer appointed, it seemed to me wise to avoid taking any one province of music (such as Form, or History, or Appreciation) and treating it in detail, for such tasks would surely be undertaken by later lecturers. My aim was rather to point out to those interested in music how wide was the range and scope of the art, and how, far from being a mere adjunct of pleasure, it might well be an integral part of the life of intellectual men.

It is a presumptuous task for any one to attempt, and I can only plead, in condonation of my arrogance in attempting it, that I think it was a task which needed to be done, that no one has ever (so far as I know) tried to do it, and that the more unsatisfactory my own essay may prove the greater will be the spur to others to provide musicians with a more competent substitute.

I have compressed some passages of the original lectures and extended others, and have also omitted entirely a lecture on 'Programme Music' which I included at Glasgow, since its interest naturally depended mainly on its illustrations. In its place

I have inserted a plea for the study of Psychology by musicians, in which many old pupils will recognize exhortations delivered to them, I hope not *ad nauseam*, in their younger days. Possibly the truths they embody will seem now, in the light of experience and riper years, to be more in touch with actual life than they did in those less serious student days.

P. C. B.

HARROW, 1923.

I

THE RAW MATERIAL OF MUSIC

A FAMOUS general is reported to have said, during the Great War, that if M. Capablanca could be persuaded to apply to the problems of strategy and tactics the genius which had made him invincible on the chessboard, then the side at whose disposal he placed himself would 'win in a week'. The story may be apocryphal, but it will serve as an introduction to these lectures, since my main object is, in the course of them, to recall and try to re-establish certain truisms which, in the hurry of to-day, seem to be slipping out of the world's memory. And one of the truisms—though at first sight it may seem to have small connexion with my anecdote—is, that the better you understand a thing the greater will be your chance of appreciating it.

There can be no doubt that we are, at the present time, in danger of dividing up knowledge into water-tight compartments, and leaving each of these to its expert. The experts retaliate on us by inventing a jargon we cannot understand, and playing an intellectual game amongst themselves ; often even boasting openly of their subject that, to paraphrase Lord Melbourne, 'there is no damned nonsense about utility in it'.

Personally, I believe this attitude of the expert to be entirely wrong. First, however useful technical terms may be, any expert ought to be able to explain his subject, in principle if not in detail, so that the average intelligent man can grasp what is being thought on that subject by those who are specializing in it. It is very useful to me, for instance, in discussing music with another specialist, to be able to use such a word as 'Tonality'. The mere existence of the word saves us many minutes' talking. But if I say that I cannot satisfy your curiosity as to what the problems of tonality involve, although you are willing to give me your attention, then I am simply confessing that I believe myself to be incompetent in explanation. Secondly, all intellectual problems that are not entirely futile have their bearing on practical life. The problems of metaphysics, ethics, logic, psychology, aesthetics, acoustics, and what not, can be and should be stated in language that will enable the same average intelligent man to know where we start from, what principles have been, by common consent, adopted or discarded, and along what road the immediate future seems to lie.

Yet the expert still loves to surround himself with a ring-fence, inside which he and his friends can play. with their abstractions, indifferent to a world clamouring for the application of thought to life. Just as the chess-master, acquiring an almost uncanny power of anticipating and guarding against every conceivable contingency, restricts his skill to a game and aims at no wider application, so the writers on, to take a single instance, aesthetics—the science of beauty—have filled our shelves with interminable volumes of abstract discussions, no one of which has ever helped a single soul to enjoy any work of art one whit the better.

If, then, you will accept my axiom that appreciation depends on understanding—and it will be presented for your acceptance more than once before my lectures are finished—you will wish to acquire from me any insight I am able to offer you into the problems that lie behind music, so that your appreciation of the art may increase in fullness and depth. And as it is always wisest and most logical to begin at the beginning, I am going to ask you first to consider the raw material which is the basis of music, which is involved in every note of music you have ever heard, without which the

whole art of music would be non-existent and inconceivable : that is to say, the phenomenon of sound.

When a man receives a blow the occurrence may be
described from any one of many points of view. We
might ask a lawyer for a legal opinion on the assault,
a boxing expert for a technical description of the hit,
a doctor for an appreciation of the damage, a moralist
for a homily on self-control. But if we ask a psychologist for a detailed description of the incident as it
strikes him *qua* psychologist, he will tell us that the
blow itself was a *stimulus*, that the recipient then
experienced an immediate *sensation*, followed at once
(unless it was a knock-out blow) by the *perception* of
the nature and cause of the sensation, and followed
later by workings of the mind, which are called *concepts*,
on the facts presented.

When we listen to music exactly the same process
occurs. Something acts as a stimulus to our auditory
nerve, producing the sensation of sound : there follows
the perception of its nature, and we say to ourselves
that it is a clarinet, or a barrel-organ, or C sharp;
and the mind is immediately provided with material
for concepts, and we pass into the realms of discrimination, memory, association, and so forth. The science
of the raw material of music (i. e. sound) is called
acoustics ; and if we look for the application of
acoustics to the above analysis we can see at once
where it is involved. The whole question of the
stimulus is a matter for purely acoustical investiga-
tion ; the question of sensation is partly acoustical and
partly physiological ; the questions of perception and
concepts lie entirely outside acoustics.

In one important respect the action of the stimulus
in the case of sound differs from the blow given and
received in the above example. For in the case of
the blow the sensation is produced by direct impact;

whereas in the case of sound the actual cause of the sensation may be many miles away. But it is quite easy to eliminate this difference by imagining a case where two comrades stand together and one of them is hit by a bullet, the other merely hearing the report of the rifle. In the case of the man who is hit we can analyse the whole incident in certain water-tight compartments. There is

1. The producing cause (the rifle), involving a study of mechanisms and explosives ;
2. The conveyance of the bullet from the rifle to the victim, involving a study of the trajectory of projectiles ;
3. The impact of the bullet, as a stimulus-producing sensation ;
4. The subsequent effects, which bring the realization of disablement, the suggestion of self-preservation, and the vision of stretchers, bandages, and hospital.

The immediate interest of the wounded man would not, of course, embrace any such analysis, and his grasp of the situation would be summed up in the words, ' I've been hit '. Similarly, his companion's comment on the incident, as far as it affects the question of sound, would be the simple statement, ' I heard the shot '. But the acoustical analysis of his experience falls into four precisely parallel divisions :

1. The producing cause of the vibrations—i. e. the explosion.
2. The conveyance of those vibrations through the air to the auditory nerve of the recipient.
3. The impact of the vibrations, producing the sensation of sound.
4. The subsequent effects, which enable the listener to deduce the nature of the weapon, the range and direction of fire, and any other facts which

an expert may be able to determine from the characteristics of the sound heard.

It is to the first three of these four divisions that we have to confine our attention now, and I want you to keep clear in your minds that every time you hear a sound, musical or otherwise, the same three divisions apply. Some one knocks at the front door; then the knocker is the producing cause; the vibrations are conveyed to your ears, wherever you may be; you then ' hear ', i. e. something in your head transforms the vibrations into sound. If you then say ' that is the postman ', your deduction may be true, but it is not acoustical, being one of the ' subsequent effects ' of division four. Similarly, every time you hear a musical sound there is the producing cause (or musical instrument), the conveyance of the ' sound ' between it and your ear, the sensation of sound inside you.

I. Let us first examine the instrument. All sound is the result of something vibrating—i. e. oscillating to and fro. If you stop the vibration the sound ceases; a fact which you have all sometimes proved by placing your finger on a tumbler which was ' ringing '. This is the first of four fundamental facts which I want you to grasp: not only that vibrations are the cause of sounds, but that there is no other cause, and that whenever there is a sound anywhere in the world there is some body-in-vibration immediately responsible for it.

The next important fact is this: that it has been discovered that all musical sounds (i. e. all sounds, even unpleasant ones, that have definite pitch) are caused by regular or ' periodic ' vibrations. The two usual and most interesting ways of proving this are called the ' graphic method ' and ' Koenig's flames '[1].

[1] By the kindness of Professor J. G. Gray and Dr. G. E. Allan (who performed the experiments) the audience at Glasgow were enabled to see the working of these and subsequent illustrations.

(*a*) *The graphic method.* A needle is attached to one prong of a tuning-fork. The fork is made to vibrate, and the needle placed perpendicularly over a strip of blackened glass, touching it. The glass is then moved along at a uniform pace, and the needle

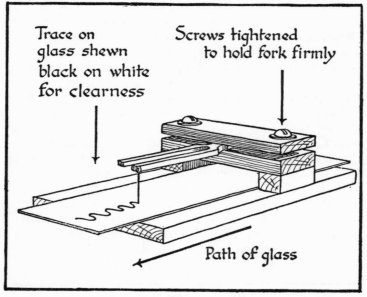

Trace on glass shewn black on white for clearness

Screws tightened to hold fork firmly

Path of glass

Fig. 1

scratches a curve as the prong vibrates. The 'waves' of this curve prove to be of uniform length, thus proving that the vibrations all take the same time, i. e. are 'periodic' (fig. 1).

(*b*) *Koenig's flames.* The gas-jet at *A* is supplied with gas through *B*. There is a partition of membrane from *D* to *E*, so that the gas from *B* can only escape at *A*. A note sung near *C* will make the membrane vibrate in sympathy with it, and each backward and forward movement of the membrane will make the flame rise or fall as it forces the gas towards the flame or pulls it in the opposite direction. This up-and-down motion of the flame, being too rapid for the eye to see, can be reflected in a revolving mirror. A noise produces in the mirror a series of jagged flames of all

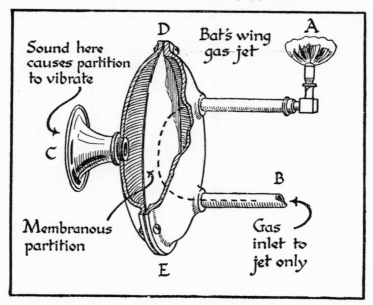

Sound here causes partition to vibrate

D

Bat's wing gas jet

A

C

Membranous partition

B

Gas inlet to jet only

E

FIG. 2

sizes and shapes, but a note of definite pitch produces a series of smooth and symmetrical flames (fig. 2).

The third important fact is that the pitch of a sound depends solely on the rapidity of the vibrations producing it : the more rapid the vibrations, the higher the pitch. And there are two curious points in connexion with pitch which you should know. First, the ' limits of hearing ' differ in different people. If I get an instrument to vibrate more and more slowly, the note it produces sinks deeper and deeper, and if I ask you to put up your hands at the moment you cease to hear anything at all—i. e. when, for you, there is absolute silence—you will put up your hands at different times. There will, that is, be a moment when half of you hear a sound which is quite inaudible to the other half. And when the vibrations get down to about 20 per second, none of you will hear anything. Similarly, if I make the rate of vibration increase, and the note becomes higher and higher, you will cease to hear anything at different moments, until at about 38,000 per second there will be silence for all of us.

The other point is, that though we can hear a sound between those limits of 20 and 38,000 vibrations per second, we cannot distinguish 'pitch' outside the restricted range of 30–4,000. In some cases the range of audibility is even narrower, and I do not know that a reasonable restriction—even one well below the average—is a great disadvantage. There are certainly notes, both high and low, on any large organ which to me have no pitch at all, and I would never make a wager as to the two or three notes at either end of a piano; but I am not convinced that I suffer any real loss from the fact.

The toothed wheel and the siren are the principal instruments used in experimenting with pitch.

(*a*) Fig. 3 explains itself as a circular disc with equidistant teeth. A motor makes it revolve at any number of revolutions per minute that we desire. A strip of metal, clamped to the table, is so placed that every tooth of the wheel depresses it, and its elasticity brings it back to be depressed again by the next tooth. Each up and down movement of the metal causes one vibration in the air. Thus, if there are 100 teeth, and the disc revolves twice per second, we get a note whose vibration-number is 200 per second, and it is invariably of the same pitch.

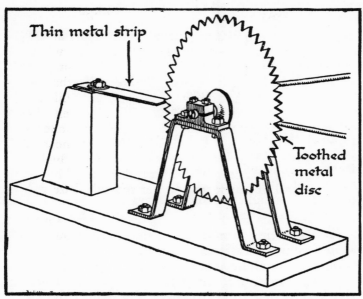

Fig. 3

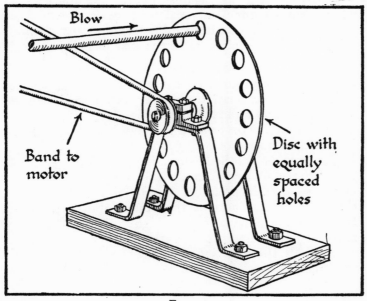

Fig. 4

B

(*b*) The siren, Fig. 4, is of exactly the same nature as the toothed wheel, with equidistant holes instead of teeth. We set it in motion and blow through a glass tube so that puffs of air get through each hole as it passes the end of the tube.

In the very earliest stages of primitive civilization, human beings try to construct something that will produce vibrations for them. They do this long before they have discovered any of the elementary facts of sound which we have been examining. And before long they find out that there are six ways of producing sound, to which six ways we, advanced as we think ourselves, are still restricted. These are :

(*a*) By setting in motion a definite ' column of air ', as in a penny whistle or an organ pipe.

(*b*) By stretching strings, as in a violin.

(*c*) By reeds, i.e. by getting strips of metal or elastic substance to beat periodically against the air.

(*d*) By forcing air against elastic membranes, as when we make our own vocal cords vibrate.

(*e*) By striking elastic membranes, as in the drum.

(*f*) By striking solids, as in the case of bells.

The last of the four facts is perhaps the most far-reaching in importance, because it is the bedrock on which all stable relationships between notes, such as we find in keys and scales, are founded. It was discovered that if you double the number of vibrations producing a note, you will produce the octave higher. If the siren or toothed wheel is producing a note of 100 vibrations per second, and we speed up the motor so that it produces a note of 200 vibrations, then the second note is the octave above the first. If we want a note an octave higher than the second note, we must get 400 vibrations. And in some of your minds the question must have arisen already as to what happens when we get the siren to produce

300 vibrations per second. That is the kind of question which the slow-witted person is apt to call 'idle curiosity'; but all advancement in knowledge is due to such questions. The answer is that we get the interval of a fifth above the note of 200 vibrations. For example, if I make a siren produce 250 vibrations per second you will hear a note in the region of 'middle C'. Increase the 250 to 500, and the note changes to the octave higher, i.e. C in the third space of the treble stave. Increase the 500 to 750, and the note is the G above that, and 1,000 vibrations produce the C that requires two leger lines.

So that if four sirens, all in action together, produce four sets of vibrations at the speed of 250, 500, 750,

Ex. 5

and 1,000, we hear a chord of four notes, as in Ex. 5 ; and when I add that if we multiply 250 by 5, and get another siren to produce 1,250 vibrations per second, the note will prove to be E, you will see that by simple multiplication you can produce the major common chord on any note, and also that you will have laid the foundations for the whole science of music.

It did not take long to discover that, in applying this principle to strings and pipes (the two earliest forms of musical instruments to be constructed), the process had to be *inverted*, i.e. where we had multiplied we had to divide. If a pipe or a string produce a certain note, you must make them *half as long* if you want the note that is an octave higher. I suppose you all know that the long organ pipes produce the deep bass notes, i.e. that the more inches in the pipe the fewer will be the vibrations it produces; but

probably few of you know that a pipe of 4 feet produces the note exactly an octave above that of an
8-foot pipe. And you all know that when a violinist is
playing the E on his top string, and wants a higher
note, he has to put down a finger of his left hand,
i. e. he has to shorten the string ; but I have met
many accomplished violinists who did not know that
to produce the octave above that E they must put the
finger down exactly half-way.

There is one interesting fact that you ought to
know about intensity, which is the scientific term for
loudness. Suppose I had a magic-lantern which threw
a patch of light one yard square on to a sheet. You
will agree that if I put the lantern twice as far away
from the sheet, then the sides of the square, instead
of being *one* yard, will be *two*, i. e. there will be an
area of four square yards on the sheet instead of one.
And if I treble the distance, the area will be nine
square yards, because the sides of the square will
be three yards each. In scientific language we say
that ' the area of light varies as the square of the
distance '. If you multiply the distance by 2, you
multiply the area by 4 ; if the distance by 3, then
the area by 9, &c.

Now if you think about it you will see that the
actual light which has, in the last case, to illuminate
an area of nine square yards is the same in quantity
as that which in the first case had to illuminate only
one square yard. Hence it will be only one-ninth as
powerful. It is just the same as with bread and butter :
if you spread a pat of butter over nine square inches of
bread it will be one-ninth as thick as when you spread
it over one square inch. If you grasp this you will
not find it impossible to understand what scientists
mean when they say that the intensity of light ' varies
inversely as the square of the distance '; for it just
means that if you multiply the distance by 2 the light

is a quarter (i. e. $\frac{1}{2^2}$) as strong ; if you multiply by 3, the light is a ninth (i. e. $\frac{1}{3^2}$) as strong.

Exactly the same is true of sound.   You might think it was common sense to say that to those of you who are 30 yards from me my voice is half as powerful as to those who are only 15 yards off.   But really, if you were all 30 yards away I should have to speak four times as loud to get the same results as if you were all only 15 yards distant.   For, just as in the case of light, the vibrations that leave my mouth have to cover an area which, at twice the distance, is four times as large, and so your individual ears will receive vibrations of one-fourth the intensity.   This is a fact which all speakers and singers should know, and one which is also useful to listeners.   If you find the band at the seaside is too loud for you, and move to a seat twice as far away, the band will sound only a quarter as loud.

II.   The second of the three divisions of the subject which I asked you to keep distinct in your mind deals with the conveyance of sound.   What happens between my mouth and your ears at this moment, or between the cause of any sound and the recipient of the sensation?

It is necessary at this point that you should try to form a conception of sound which will be new and perhaps almost incredible to most of you, but which, nevertheless, is the absolutely true conception, and not in any way the mere bewildering hypothesis that it may seem to those of you who have had no scientific training.

When we say that anything is ' sounding ' we are not really speaking accurately.   The only thing that any ' sound-producer ' does is to produce vibrations. When you force wind through an organ-pipe, or draw a bow across a violin-string, or clap your hands, you cause a disturbance in the air, and that disturbance travels, in the form of air-vibrations, until it meets with an apparatus (such as your ears) constructed to receive the vibrations and transmit them to a brain, which then turns them into sound. Before a sound can be said to exist there *must* be three things : (*a*) a vibrating body, such as my vocal cords, (*b*) a transmitting medium, such as the air between you and me, and (*c*) the brain, which turns the vibrations of my voice into sound for you. If I made no vibrations you would hear nothing ; if this room could suddenly be made a vacuum, by having all the air exhausted from it, I could go on talking for some seconds, exactly as I am doing now, but you would hear nothing at all, since the air is our means of contact ; if every one in this room, including myself, were stone-deaf, I could go on talking, and shout as vigorously as I liked, but there would be dead silence in the room, because none of the vibrations could find an apparatus to transform them into sound.

Let me quote a more striking illustration :

‘ If you go alone to the organ in an empty church,
‘ pull out all the stops, fix down all the notes, and
‘ turn on the wind, the result will be a noise best left
‘ to the imagination. Then go and stand outside the
‘ church, leaving it empty as you found it. You will
‘ still hear the organ, but in the church itself there is
‘ *perfect silence*. The organ-pipes are vibrating and
‘ are doing nothing else ; the air is passing on those
‘ vibrations to the nearest ear, and is doing nothing
‘ else ; and the first *sound* in connexion with the whole
‘ affair arises at the moment when, and the place
‘ where, the vibrations come in contact with a living
‘ apparatus designed to receive and translate them.’

I know that to some of you this may seem to be nonsense. You will think it mere juggling with words to be told that a deaf bugler, bursting his lungs by himself in the middle of a desert island, is not in any way disturbing the peace of nature because he is not making any noise at all. But it is the simple truth, which you should try to apprehend, that the only function of the sound-producer is to create vibrations which will, if they can reach a living brain, then for the first time change from vibrations into sound.

The only other point of importance I am going to tell you about, in connexion with the medium, is this. We all think of air, and air alone, as the medium for vibrations ; but there are innumerable media, and many of them are far better for the purpose than air. If a felled tree, for instance, is lying on the ground, and you place your ear at one end while somebody gently scratches the other end with a penknife, you will hear the scratching with ease ; but if you take your ear away from the tree and then listen—i. e. rely on the air as the medium instead of the wood—you will hear nothing. Nor is the air the best medium in the way of speed. Sound travels in air roughly at about 1,100 feet per second,[1] but in water its velocity is nearly 5,000 (a fact of immense importance in the submarine campaign), in wood (along the grain) from 10,000 to 15,000, in metals, such as iron and steel, over 16,000.

Most of the sound, however, that you and I will ever have to deal with comes to us through the air. And it is interesting to know that vibrations in the air, when they strike against anything hard are reflected from it, and when they meet anything soft are destroyed. An echo, for example, is the result of vibrations hitting something firm and ' bouncing back' like a tennis-ball from a wall. If you found a place where an echo existed, and hung a thick or soft curtain

[1] The rate is really 1,090 feet per second at 32° Fahrenheit (i.e. at freezing-point). It increases at almost exactly 1 foot per second for each degree as the thermometer rises.

over the reflecting-surface, the 'bounce' would be killed—just as if the tennis-ball hit a net—and there would be no echo. Every singer and public speaker has at some time tried an empty room and been delighted with its resonance—i. e. with its powers of reflecting sound—only to find that the same room, filled by an audience covered with soft clothes, had no reverberation at all.

III. A musical sound has three characteristics: pitch, intensity, and quality. We have discussed pitch and intensity, and I now want to tell you how your ear distinguishes between two sounds of different quality.

It may surprise you to know that, just as nearly everything we have ever tasted is a combination of certain elements which a chemist could analyse, so almost every sound you have ever heard, even when you thought it was a single note, is a combination of other sounds. If you would like to train your ears I beg you, when you get home, go to the piano and strike the C which is two leger lines below the bass stave. Strike it hard several times, holding it down the last time, and listen attentively until it is almost inaudible. After a very few trials—possibly the first time—you will notice there is another note sounding strongly, the G in the top space of the bass stave. After a few more trials you will plainly hear the E on the bottom line of the treble stave. You will then have discovered a fact known for ages to men of science, viz. that a note is almost invariably a combination of sounds. These various sounds which combine to form a note are called the 'partial-tones' of the note, which is itself called the 'fundamental partial'.

It is just possible to get a sound that has no partials —called a 'simple' sound—just as it is possible to get a simple primary colour; but you have probably seldom heard one. The nearest approach to it is the sound of a tuning-fork struck very gently, or the soft cooing of a dove. And the fact I want you to grasp is that ' quality ' in a sound is due to the number and relative strength of the partial-tones which constitute it. They need not all be present—in fact, as the series extends upwards to the extreme limit of hearing we may safely say they are never all present. But if you get a flute, a trumpet, a violin, and a singer all to produce the same note at the same intensity, then the only difference between the four sounds is a difference of quality, which is entirely due to the fact that each of the four sounds, though their ' fundamental partial ' is the same, contains different ' upper partials '.

Ex. 6

I do not think, unless you are definitely a musical student, it is at all important for you to know more about the mysteries underlying ' quality '. But I should like to point out one fact about the ' harmonic chord ' (as it is called) in Ex. 6, lest you should think this matter of partial-tones to be mere theorizing. If you study the numbers at the side you will see that 1, 2, 4, and 8 are all an octave apart ; and if you continued the series you would find that 16, 32, and 64 were all of them the note C. Similarly 3, 6, 12, 24, &c., are all G ; 5, 10, 20, &c., always E. These facts have a practical result. For we can tell two things in consequence of them, viz. the vibration-numbers of the notes, and the length of pipe or string necessary to produce them. For instance, if we know that the bottom C of Ex. 6 has 60 vibrations per second and is produced by a pipe of 8 feet, then the vibration number of the G which is the third partial is 60 × 3, and its pipe-length is $\frac{8}{3}$ feet; similarly the vibration-number of the E which is the fifth partial is 60 × 5, and its pipe-length is $\frac{8}{5}$ feet.

If you pursue the subject of partial-tones a little farther—which you can do by studying any elementary text-book on sound—you will be initiated into some fascinating and bewildering mysteries in connexion with the ordinary major scale that you know so well. And you will learn some surprising things, such as why an expert piano-tuner is a man who is paid for putting your piano definitely out of tune. But perhaps you would rather pay in peace and leave such puzzles alone. I have just scratched the surface of the field of acoustics for you, in the hope of convincing you that it is interesting, and that by being interested in the material of which music is made, you will find your appreciation of the music itself a little more intelligent in quality, and certainly no less in quantity, than heretofore.

II

THE ORIGIN OF MUSIC AS AN ART

MOST of you will have heard it said that all true study makes use of the genetic method. And some of you, out of intellectual curiosity, will have made inquiries and discovered that this method commends the study of the genesis, or origin, of things. In plain language, if you want to understand anything properly, you must find out how it came to be what it is.

Any inquiry into the origin of music would, I think, be futile, because logically any sound of definite pitch is a musical sound, and such sounds precede the human race. So I want to talk about the origin of music *as an art*; by which I mean the earliest attempts of human beings to treat sound as a material in which they can express their feelings, following on the discovery that enjoyment could be obtained from the purposive arrangement of sounds.

When I was a young student there were two theories that held the field, sponsored by names of such eminence that musicians accepted them as the only possible alternatives, and for the most part (if interested in the matter) became partisans of one or the other. Darwin told us that the origin of our art was sex, instancing the male birds who, in the mating season, sing in competition before the female. Spencer, on the other hand, said the art arose from the deliberate attempt to reproduce the inflexions of speech. It would be absurd for any one but a biologist to join issue with such giants. But the mere musician may say, without impertinence, that we have come to look to the anthropologist, who studies mankind as a whole rather than man as an organism, for enlightenment as to the earliest practical efforts. From him we can learn what is actually being done to-day by primitive peoples, and, finding certain lines of action normal and others exceptional, can feel some assurance in piecing together the artistic history of the human race.

Thinkers have been confronted, since thinking began, with a time-worn problem as to whether thought creates language, or language creates thought. It is not, I am told, a problem of any bitterness at the present time, and we can accept the general view of thinkers that an idea precedes its name. Human beings must have known heat from cold, rain from sunshine, and have taken action due to their knowledge, long before they had invented sounds to express these things. They must have grasped what a circle was, if only from the sight of sun and moon, before setting about to find a name for it. The truth is summed up by a writer who says, ' The range of human thoughts and emotions greatly transcends the range of symbols man has invented to express them.' Leaving aside the ' human thoughts ' in the above quotation, let us consider the fact that human emotions always have been, and still are, beyond the power of exact expression in words.

How then do we, as we undoubtedly do, manage to express feeling? At first we do it unconsciously, as in the tone-colour of our voices when we say, ' Please don't do that ' ; or when the man with the artistic temperament scratches crosses with a fishbone on the handle of his stone axe to relieve his feelings. Later, finding these expressions of our feelings affect other people, we do them consciously and intentionally to produce that effect, and art—not quite purged of utilitarianism—is born. The process, to be complete, must be fourfold. I feel strongly ; my emotion finds expression in the tone-colour of my voice ; the tone-colour awakens a certain response in you ; you feel. That is the type of all art. Emotion creating expression in the artist, expression creating emotion in the audience. And what I have done by tone-colour cannot be done by the words alone. ' Cold print ' is cold because it is robbed of the persuasiveness of tone-colour. How many proposals of marriage would be accepted if the same words were addressed to the lady in a typescript ?

Art, then, is the expression of what eludes language. This definition may seem, it is true, to exclude poetry ; but I would ask you to consider what the poet does. He has something to say—let us suppose he has noticed that the light is failing and wants to say, ' It is getting dark quickly.' But he knows that the statement will not cause any emotion in his readers, so he searches for some method of saying the same thing that will, in some recondite way, touch their hearts ; and the sentence becomes, ' Fast falls the eventide.' And you must remember that, though we read poetry with the eye, it always appeals to us through its sound and rhythm—two attributes which are not visual. It is, I think you will agree, the main function of the poet to reach our feelings by means of rhythm (for all emotion tends to become rhythmical), vowel-arrangement (which is a co-ordination of pure sound), and other devices (such as, in the phrase quoted, alliteration) which have been found empirically to be successful. The plain man divines this when he says that it is the ' music ' of words, and not their ' hard sense ', that moves him, and you will admit that the poet seizes on this accidental musical element in words, and not on the primary and essential function (which is to convey meaning), when he makes his appeal to us.

Sooner or later the flash of insight comes, and some one grasps the fact that these attributes of tone-colour, rhythm, and pitch, with which words may be clothed and made to move us, are not inseparable from words. They can be used to rouse emotion without the necessity of coupling them to language and bringing in the facts of life. And when these three essentials of music are so used, singly or in combination, for the definite and conscious purpose of expressing emotion, the art of music is born.

Having discovered, then, that rhythm, tone, and pitch may be used as raw materials for a new art, certain human beings would assume the functions of composers, and experiment in every direction; and every experiment would add a little to knowledge, increase the control over the medium by developing technique, and reach a further stage in the evolution of music. But such experiments were made (and, as anthropologists tell us, are now being made amongst primitive peoples), not with the daring and adventurous enthusiasm we might expect, but with slow and cautious steps in one direction at a time. At first the experiments are always made with rhythm alone, later with melody, and latest of all with combinations of sounds which lead to the discovery of harmony.

These three stages frequently, of course, overlap; e.g. when a fairly secure grip of rhythm has been obtained experiments in melody may begin without causing the abandonment of the study of rhythm. But, generally speaking, the stages are so well marked that they are looked for with some certainty everywhere, and they have been named the ' Drum stage ', the ' Pipe stage ', and the ' Lyre stage '.

I. *The Drum stage* begins when first pure rhythm is used to give pleasure or excite emotion. Without becoming entangled in the labyrinths of the Lange-James theory we may recognize that emotion involves action. If you are angry you cannot sit still. This inevitable connexion between emotion and movement was certain to lead, sooner or later, to the discovery of the fact that rhythm (which is organized movement) could be used to excite emotion. It is said by observers that the warriors of savage tribes, before a battle, will sit on the ground while a musician with a tom-tom will play, without cessation or alteration, one reiterated elementary rhythmical figure such as

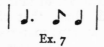

Ex. 7

At first nothing happens; after some minutes a slight but noticeable restlessness begins; ultimately the whole audience is worked into a state of frenzy, some of them even foaming at the mouth. If you find this difficult to believe, just remember how irritated you and I can become when some one continually drums a rhythm with his fingers on the breakfast table.

You all know that rhythm is, in its primary sense, the marking off of time into equal periods by means of accent. But perhaps some of you do not realize two facts of importance. First, something inside us *insists* on so dividing time, by imagining accents when they are not there. If I had here an electric riveter, which would give a series of periodic taps all accentually equal, you would every one of you find yourselves sooner or later grouping those taps mentally as ' *one* two, *one* two ' or as ' *one* two three, *one* two three '.

Secondly, we are said to be at present incapable of grouping otherwise than by twos and threes. It is impossible for us, the authorities say, to pronounce a word like ' necessary ' without putting a secondary accent on the third syllable which makes its importance greater than that of syllables two and four. It *must* become, we are told, a bar of $\frac{2}{4}$ time with four quavers in it. Similarly we cannot 'apperceive' a group of five, such as the opening phrase of Tchaikovski's well-known movement (Ex. 8), without mentally creating a secondary accent on either the third or fourth beat:

Ex. 8

We may be, and probably are, evolving into creatures with powers which at present we do not possess—a possibility that is often lost sight of when the conservatives among us condemn modern experiments. But we certainly have not yet reached the stage of development in our sense of rhythm that has been attained by some comparative savages; for we are authoritatively told that they can with ease produce and recognize combined rhythms as intricate, for example, as thirteen in combination with seventeen.

II. *The Pipe stage* begins when the first experimenter tries to construct a tune, however elementary. The cause of his experiment cannot be determined. It may be an imitation of a bird, or the accidental discovery that you can blow down a hollow pipe, or the observation of a stretched string, or (as Spencer thought) the recognition that we inflect our voices in speech. Early attempts at melody, however, are of the same character as those in the drum stage: very short and incessantly repeated. It is only by slow and tentative experiment that the main principles are discovered—such principles, for example, as that certain notes are better than others to finish on (leading to the feeling for a key-note), or that a high note is not an accident but a point of emotion (leading to a feeling for climax as an element in structure).

The chief noticeable point is this, that sooner or later some one will discover that he can make the task he is performing more pleasant by singing at it; and there are many occupations in which such singing is forced to be rhythmical. If you sing while you walk, or dance, or haul a rope, or rock a baby, you will be forced either to invent tunes which have periodic rhythm, or to impose such on the tunes you already know by heart.

There is no doubt that the first combinations of melody and rhythm arose in this way, by the accident of common need, and that melodies, after the discovery of the possibility of adapting them to practical and popular ends, fall into two classes : those with, and those without, periodic accent. And for ages these two classes will develop along separate lines, since the ' non-periodic ' composers will always look down on the melodies that are cast, as it were, into the ready-made accentual systems required by the dance or lullaby or shanty, and will look on it as a point of honour to keep their own work free from this characteristic. You will understand this if you think of plainsong, where the greatest pains were taken, even when the accents of the words were periodic (as in hymns), to prevent the rhythm of the music from hinting at any connexion with the popular dance-music of the village green.

III. *The Lyre stage* arrives when, by design or accident, it is discovered that combinations of sound are manageable. It is, of course, inconceivable that no one should ever have discovered that two simultaneous sounds might produce a pleasant effect ; but it is clear that the conception of such an effect as depending on permanent and tractable relationships between notes could not arrive until considerable progress had been made in the knowledge of scales and in the construction of instruments.

c

It is generally said that, historically, counterpoint precedes harmony. With reservations, this is true. But the first discovery that two different notes sound ' nice ' together—the beginning of the whole matter—is an harmonic discovery. And when the earliest two-part music is tried it is always said to take the form of singing a known tune in fourths—clearly an attempt to elongate the harmony which had been found pleasant. This form of singing is called ' Organum ', and you can read all about it in text-books on Musical History ; but as you may be sceptical whether human beings could ever stand anything so crude, let me tell you that in the remoter parts of Iceland they are, I believe, practising ' Organum ' to-day.

You may also wonder why such an uncouth interval as a fourth is chosen, and the answer should interest you. In talking of ' partial tones ' you will remember that, next to the fundamental, the most prominent partial is number three, whose sound is a twelfth above the prime-note. If you took my advice and tried your piano you may even have found that you cannot strike C without hearing G very prominently. Hence if you sing C, and want to make a change, G is the obvious note to change to, since it is already ringing in your head, and as it requires an effort to sing *up* to G, and your power of making an effort is, in this rudimentary stage, concentrated on getting the right note, your vocal cords will relax and you will sing *down* to the G below—a fourth. If you think this explanation far-fetched, let me tell you that the same process is followed by every baby I have ever known. For some months they do not sing notes, but ' swirl ' ; then for some months they sing single notes ; then, trying for an interval, they do not, even by accident, hit on the note above or below, or a third above or below, but invariably, in my experience, a downward fourth.

When 'Organum' is abandoned it is followed by 'Descant', or more properly the discovery of descant makes organum obsolete. Descant consists of extemporizing, and later on of deliberately composing, melodies that can be sung while a known melody is being performed. This is, of course, purely contrapuntal, and is the first real appearance of part-music as an artistic thing. From the crude beginnings of descant to the finished complexities of Byrd and Bach is one long straight line of development, as from the seed to the harvest, and the milestones in the intervening period mark progress in development rather than change in kind.

Harmony, in its modern sense of clothing a melodic note or series of notes with chords, or of providing a chord pleasant to listen to by itself, could not arrive until the key-system had developed; but the earliest attempts at harmony as an accompaniment followed rapidly on the first rough organization of tonality. It did not, as you might think, take the form of accompaniment while the melody was in progress, but of stating, at the end of a phrase, what the chord-of-rest for the moment might be.

I have myself heard two curious examples. One was, many years ago, in a remote Irish village, where a harper who had learnt from his father, who in turn had learnt from *his* father—and so on for countless generations—sang a song in the way in which, I am sure, it might have been sung five hundred years ago. The only use he made of the harp was to 'thrum' a chord, generally tonic or dominant, at the end of a phrase. The other case was in Kimberley, in 1913, when a native sat by the roadside playing a tune with a bow on a single-stringed instrument, using intervals unknown in European music. And at each important phrase-end he played a little figure of notes so rapidly as to give the impression that it was

a chord. So you must not think of the earliest harmony as an attempt to make chords do most of the
things they now do for you and me, but rather as an
expression of the dawning feeling that the mind
required ' points of rest ' as melodies increased in
length, and that a solid chord at the end of a phrase
could act as a mental milestone.

Up to this point I have talked as if the development
of music depended on the individual development of
the factors of rhythm, melody, and harmony. If, however, you look deeper, now that you have seen that
these characteristics actually did develop each along
its own lines, you will find there was a common
cause of development, and this common cause is
structure. The human mind, before it can grip
anything, *must* discover some plan in it. None of us
would ever have mastered our multiplication-tables if
we had learnt the 144 facts in a random order ; our
history is divided into reigns and centuries, our verbs
into moods and tenses ; and our minds, discerning
system, classify and grasp the significance of details.
Lest you should think this statement purely doctrinaire, take a simple illustration. Suppose a plain
bare wall of a room had to be painted, and you found
an entirely inartistic person, gave him a pot of blue
and another of red paint, and set him to work. Is it
conceivable, even if he were a lunatic from the asylum,
that he would straightway dip his brush in the paint-
pot and splash the wall haphazard? His first plans
would be practical : he would see that he must have
steps to reach the ceiling, and a floor-cloth to save the
carpet. Then he would consider his scheme—that is
to say, he would evolve some plan for using his two
colours. A very crude painter might be content with
dividing the wall in the middle and painting one half
blue, the other red. If slightly more ambitious, he

might try stripes. A more imaginative mind would think of squares and circles, or conventional patterns, or might even, if he had any real artistic instinct, venture on red roses on a blue ground or blue delphiniums on a red one. But I cannot believe any sane man, woman, or child would begin painting entirely without intention and purpose.

The human mind, then, demands at least a minimum of coherence and system, and once given systematic coherence can grasp ideas of ever-increasing complexity. It is clear, for instance, that in the case of the reiterated rhythmical figure on the tom-tom there is a limit-of-memory to what the mind can retain. Make your figure too long and you will not discern at what point the repetition begins. Similarly with a melodic phrase; when it is unduly lengthy there comes a point (as in an exceptionally long sentence in a speech) where we lose our bearings and are left ' in the air '. And the only possibility of our keeping a mental hold on anything but the shortest musical phrase, or the shortest sentence of conversation, lies in the power of its creator, acquired slowly in the course of many experiments, to make it logically coherent, i. e. to satisfy the demand of the mind for structure.

The power of the mind, then, to hold successive impressions and to piece them together, depends on the presence of plan or structure in the material presented. For music is a panorama and the apprehension of a phrase—even one of two notes—is a feat of memory, since the first note is in the past as soon as the second becomes present. At first the ' unit ' is the single note, and we cannot piece together a phrase any better than the child who, after reading aloud painfully and slowly, ' The cat is on the mat ', has no idea of what the sentence means until, *after* saying it, he comes to think about it.

In the course of these lectures I want to impress on you that the bedrock condition underlying all understanding and appreciation of music is the grasp of its structure. Not the acquisition of an arsenal of technical terms, like ' episode ', ' working-out ', ' re-capitulation ', and the rest, which make most analytical programmes so dreary to you ; these will come in time, when you have grasped the idea and want a nickname for it. But rather the realization of the fact that the only reason your mind can get hold of the simplest tune, such as ' Auld Lang Syne ', is that the tune is ' organized '. Tap it on the table, and you will find its rhythmical structure ; write it out on a stave and you will see the melody has the simplest of objects, for it climbs gradually and gracefully to its highest note at its central point, and then with dignity travels home again.

If you feel uncertain as to what is meant by ' harmonic structure ', try all the chords you can think of to accompany the top note and the final note, and think why most of them—all but one, I should say, in each case—are unsatisfactory. The only answer can be that a wrong chord is wrong because, using that chord, you ' don't know where you are ', and this means that, ignorant as you may be of harmonic theory, your mind, nevertheless, has made an harmonic demand.

The application of rhythmical structure to the single melodic line does not reach, as in the pure rhythm combinations of 13 and 17, a stage of great complexity. Being limited, as I said, by the power of memory, the point very soon arrives where rhythm is no longer an appeal to the feelings but becomes an exercise of the mathematical faculty. In the case of melodic development, however, another considera-tion arises which is of immense, though not at first obvious, importance. Melodic phrases, whether sung or played on a pipe, are limited by the necessity of taking breath. At first the phrase to be repeated will be very short, because the inventiveness of man is capable of no more. But as this improved, phrases become longer ; always, however, being limited by the necessity of breathing. Gradually, in the course of this stage, arises the feeling that a certain note is the right one to end on ; not necessarily always the same note, but a note whose position seems to be demanded by the nature of the phrase. It is what we nowadays would call a feeling for a ' tonic ' or key-note.

Ultimately, however, there will come a time when the phrase-maker desires to extend his tune beyond the limits of one breath. But the fact that he *must* breathe will make it imperative for him to have a temporary halt somewhere. If he uses his key-note at this place, then he has reached home, so to speak, and to continue would be merely to add a second phrase. This he undoubtedly did, in many cases, but the process is one of simple addition and not of structural development. The latter occurs when the composer found that there were notes on which he could rest temporarily without giving the impression of finality, and without making the listener ' lose the thread '. It was the discovery of punctuation in music ; the invention of the ' cadence ', the means by which the skilful tune-maker can elongate his melody to almost any length, logically and convincingly. And it has survived to the present day, explaining what so modern a critic as Mr. Ernest Newman means when he says, ' All phrasing is primarily vocal '.

When once the extended phrase was possible, and the mind had learnt to hold the panorama in memory, other devices became obvious, such as repetition (cf. ' Three Blind Mice ') and sequence (cf. ' All Through

the Night'). But the most important development
that took place after the combination of rhythm and
melody was, from the modern point of view, the
discovery of bar-rhythm by the ' popular ' musicians.

The music of the learned was always, until comparatively modern times, on the model of prose.
Even in hymn-tunes, where the words suggest equal
and symmetrical phrases of music, pains were taken to
avoid identical accentual patterns. But dance music
and folk-songs were not so sophisticated; the music
fell into a fore-ordained rhythmical mould. And
there grew up the realization that besides the primary
rhythm within the bar (such as the rhythm of the
first bar of ' Auld Lang Syne ') there was a secondary
rhythm composed of the first beats of all the bars
that constituted a phrase. Take, for instance, the
hymn-tune ' St. Anne ' ('O God, our help in ages
past '). Play it through, making the last note of the
second line a minim instead of a dotted semibreve.
The unsatisfactory result is the same as if you made
a line of poetry two syllables short ; your mind feels
it has been put ' out of step ' ; in other words, the
bar-rhythm has been destroyed. Musicians know how
the normal feeling for four-bar rhythm led composers
to discover the *curiosa felicitas* of three- and five-
bar phrases, and all the complexities of syncopation
and cross-accent.

Ex. 9

Of the development of harmony I shall speak to
you in a later lecture. Here I want you to realize
that harmony was originally a static and not a dynamic
thing. The first view of it was perpendicular and not

horizontal, for the attempts at organum were attempts to carry *one* pleasant combination along a line of varying pitch, and not attempts to link together two harmonic combinations. Many centuries elapsed after the discovery of the pleasantness of a ' chord ' before the ability arose to write the succession of chords in Ex. 9, and when composers had acquired that ability they had left the origin of music as an art far behind them.

III

THE NATURE OF BEAUTY

THE title of this lecture will, to a great majority of people, seem so forbidding that I feel it needs a justification, if not an apology. Art aims at creating the impression of beauty, as every one admits when, by calling things ugly, they deny them artistic excellence. Yet as soon as you put to any one the question ' What is beauty ? ' you will find that, almost invariably, the question is considered a foolish one, since everybody uses the word and everybody knows what it means. It is, nevertheless, a question which the deepest thinkers have been puzzling over from time immemorial, and though, no doubt, some of them have thought that they had caught the will-o'-the-wisp, they have been, one and all, singularly unable to prove their success in intelligible language.

All discovery is founded on curiosity. Even accidental discoveries would pass unheeded if somebody did not (like Newton with the apple) ' wonder why ' And the first invariable custom of primitive man is, when seeking the cause of anything, to take refuge in personification. He feels a certain emotion and invents some one as the cause of it—in technical language he is said to ' reïfy ' it. The woods at night frighten him, so he creates a spirit of the woods ; insanity passes his understanding, so he says the insane are possessed by devils ; until he has at last provided himself with a hierarchy of quasi-deities and lulled himself into the habit of attributing all things to causes outside himself and outside his control.

Consequently it seemed obvious, and would seem

obvious to you and me if we were a little more primitive
than we are, that beauty was entirely a property of
the thing we called beautiful. It was beautiful
because it possessed beauty; and if it was not beautiful
you might make it so by adding beauty to it just as
you mix sugar with pudding to make it sweet.

I should be the last person to say anything disrespectful, especially in Scotland, about metaphysics,
since I firmly believe that a knowledge of metaphysics,
even if it is as small as my own, is the greatest incentive
to clear thinking. But in this matter of beauty I think
no one can say that the metaphysicians have helped
us much. And though it may be rash for a non-
philosopher to say so, I venture to think the reason of
their failure lies in the fact that they have never got
away from the attitude of primitive man. To them
beauty is always a property of the object and nothing
else, and their quest of it through innumerable
centuries has been so unsuccessful that even now
none of them have coaxed it from its hiding-place.

If, however, you have followed, however distantly,
the course of thought through the last few decades,
you will know that its whole procedure, both in aim
and methods, has been changed by the rise of modern
psychology. To the psychologist this tendency to
reïfy is the stumbling-block to all knowledge. To him
the central fact is human reaction. An object, present
or remote (which means outside the range of actual
contact with the senses), is perceived by a subject,
and in the reaction of the subject lies the field of
attainable knowledge. Thus to the psychologist
' beauty ', as an entity, has no existence *per se*. But
when a certain thing is the cause of a certain effect
in us we say we have an impression of sweetness or
softness or beauty; and that since these effects,
previous to our reaction, had no more existence than
a sound has previous to the effect of vibrations on

a brain, it is manifestly absurd to reïfy the effect and
call it a cause.

If the above is a fair description of the quarrel
between metaphysician and psychologist—and I think
it is—we may say, without arrogating to ourselves the
function of arbiter between them, that the examination of our own reactions does seem, to musicians at
all events, to present some possibilities of getting
a little insight into the problems of the beautiful.   If
Cambridge wins the boat-race the Oxford man feels
sad, and may well wish, if he is of a speculative turn
of mind, to find out what type of cause produces the
effect of sadness in him.   But to look for the sadness
in the boat-race, or to say it resides in the result,
seems to the plain man to be deliberately placing the
specimen where the microscope cannot reach it.   We
know that we feel, we know that art works on our
power of feeling, and we know that when we feel in
a certain way we say, proleptically, that the cause of
the feeling is beautiful ; and there should be a reasonable chance of arriving at some consensus of opinion
as to what qualities are essential in an object if this
particular reaction is to follow in us.

First of all, let us be clear as to the meaning we
attach to the words ' feeling ' and ' emotion '.   We
are all apt, and even accredited psychologists are
sometimes little better, to use the words in a loose
overlapping way.   Emotions are the definite qualities
coupled with the instincts.   Fear, for example, is the
emotion accompanying the instinct of self-preservation,
anger that accompanying the instinct of pugnacity,
amusement that accompanying the instinct of laughter.
' Feeling ' is something quite different.   It has only
two qualities, pleasure and pain ; that is to say, we
know whether we wish to increase or diminish the
intensity of our feeling, since it is nearly always on

either the pleasant or unpleasant side. Both qualities can be present together, as when we deliberately press on an aching tooth, or suck a lemon, in which cases we know that the pleasure comes from the pain, and judge that the agreeable outweighs the disagreeable; when the balance turns the activity ceases. Every emotion has a feeling-tone, as it is called : amusement is pleasurable, anger painful ; but the feeling is not the emotion, nor the emotion the feeling, though in conversation we confuse the two and call a person emotional if his feelings are easily affected.

Now if I wish to communicate with you, I can only approach you through your senses ; if these are shut off from me I can no more get into contact with you than a lemon can get into contact with a logarithm. But if I am able to appeal to you through your senses, then my appeal must be either to your understanding or to your feelings. I may say ' It 's ten o'clock ', or I may utter a cry of distress that will affect your feelings even before you realize what it signifies. Innumerable sciences (such as grammar, logic, and the rest) have grown up which are concerned with the appeal to the understanding. But though the appeal *direct* to the feelings is rare, they can, nevertheless, be reached without the intervention of the understanding ; as when a sudden clap of thunder, rousing our instinct of self-preservation, causes the painful feeling, however much under control, of fear, or when a beautiful sunset, rousing the instinct of self-abasement, causes the pleasurable feeling of humility.

Art, you will agree, must in the end reach our feelings, since a work of art which leaves us completely unmoved is, for us, no work of art at all. We may apply to it some preconceived critical apparatus and discourse learnedly on its excellences or shortcomings, but if we are entirely unaffected by it—if we find we have to say ' it leaves me cold '—then the contact between its creator and us has not been made, and if you will pardon an expressive colloquialism, the whole proceeding is a ' wash out '—only, remember, so far as *you* are concerned, since your neighbour may be intensely moved. Our inquiry then becomes an attempt to answer the question, ' How does art reach our feelings ? ' Does it, like the thunder, awaken a primitive instinct with its concomitant emotion, or does it find some other path to them ? The answer is that art reaches our feelings always *through* the understanding. It is not, like logic and grammar, an appeal *to* the understanding, but aims at a goal whose only approach is *through* the understanding. And since this conception of art seems to me to be fundamental, I will try to show you the grounds on which it rests.

Imagine some particular thing that gives you pleasure : let us say a note on the clarinet, or a line of poetry such as ' Home they brought her warrior dead '. You admit that either of these instantaneously changes, however slightly, the ' quality ' of your feeling, and you find, if you try to give a reason, that you have embarked on a long and vague explanation which, in the end, does not satisfy even yourself.

Suppose, however, that you make an experiment, and change the relationship of the constituents in each case. Alter the arrangement of partial-tones that gave the clarinet-quality to the sound ; imagine the line of poetry to be ' They brought her warrior home dead '. The state of your feelings will also change in the direction of greater or less pleasure. And it is this fact that is implied in the definition, so cryptic to the uninitiated, that ' all beauty is relative '. It comes like a cold douche to the enraptured beauty-seeker to be told that the effect of things on him is due to the ' relationship of the constituents ', and he suspects that you, deserted by the gods and deprived of the power of feeling that thrill which beauty brings to him, are trying to entangle him in the morass of mathematical formulae.   Yet the statement, in all its cold-bloodedness, is true.   By tampering with the partial tones of the clarinet it would be quite easy to make you call the sound ugly ; and if the clarinet played a tune, and you called the melody, as distinct from the tone, a beautiful one, any alteration in the relative position of the notes will modify your verdict.

Consider a simpler case.   You enter an empty apartment and exclaim 'What a beautiful room !' The room next door, if an exact reproduction, produces an effect only lessened because the element of surprise is absent.   If you then enter a third empty room and exclaim ' Not nearly so beautiful ', is there anything to account for your change of feeling except a difference in its proportions—i. e. in the relationship of its parts ?   Similarly with such things as tables, chairs, and carpets, with which a room is furnished, the beauty of each depends on relations within itself. And the effect of a room where every piece of furniture is in itself beautiful may be (and often is) ugly, while the effect of another where all the furniture is ugly (so long as it is not ugly enough to distract your attention from the room as a whole) may be beautiful. And this is the meaning of the rather hard saying that ' beauty is relative '.

If you grant the truth of this conception of beauty you will find little difficulty in accepting my premiss that art appeals to the feelings through the under-standing, since relationships between any things what-ever are apprehended by the understanding and not by the feelings.   Certain relationships produce a state of feeling in you which is modified by a change in the relationships ; which means that ' you ' have discriminated between the two things presented to you.   But it is only your understanding which can discriminate, and your change of feeling is the result of the discrimination.

There remains the question of the intensity with which we react, and I think we shall all agree that our experiences are identical in process, although we do not react with the same intensity to the same stimuli. If I hear a series of melodies I may say that I rather like the first, the second better, the third a good deal, and so on. My pleasure in them increases steadily, if they happen to be placed in the right order. At last there comes a melody which gives me so intense a pleasure that I am ' taken out of myself ', as we say, and am so deeply moved that I almost feel I have handed over my self-control to, and am dominated by, some outside influence. I suppose all of you will admit that art has at some time had this intense effect on you. The Greeks called this transcendent moment *catharsis,* for we feel we are undergoing a kind of purification. The earlier melodies gave me pleasure, each seeming ' more ' beautiful than the last, but the final experience seems to bring me into the presence of perfect beauty. I can safely use the word in this sense now, for you know that I am reïfying in order to be intelligible, and that all the time I am aware that the process under examination has taken place in me. It was *I* who had the feeling of pleasure, it was *my* feeling that grew more and more intense until the moment when I can only express it by saying that any feeling of pleasure has been transmuted into a feeling of beauty.

I used, just now, the phrase ' more beautiful ', and there is a difficulty in connexion with it which brings a fog into many minds. People are always to be found disputing whether one thing is more beautiful than another, and the argument generally ends with a shrug of the shoulders and a quotation of the old tag, ' De gustibus non est disputandum '.

There can be, of course, no certainty that what appeals to your taste appeals to mine; but I should like you to see that the discussion of matters of taste can nevertheless be profitable if we once recognize the limitation which this truism involves. If you love oranges and hate lemons, and I like lemons and detest oranges, any discussion between us as to which is the 'nicer' is ruled out by the facts of the case. It is a question which is never going to be settled in this world or any other, and no one could be in the least happier if an irrevocable decision were given. But there *is* a point we might discuss (but probably would be too acrimonious to think of) which has a really practical importance, and is the only consideration that matters to anybody: what constitutes the difference between a good and bad orange, or a good and bad lemon? You may think a discussion on these lines, leaving less room for personal dogmatism, might prove rather a tame combat, but, if you think how a Chinaman is said to prefer his eggs, you will see there are still a good many first principles to be agreed upon; and you will have the satisfaction of knowing that on no other lines can the argument clear the air at all.

Yet every musician must have listened time and again to disputes—it would be too complimentary to call them arguments—whether symphonies are nobler things than symphonic poems, or whether the fugue is a higher form of composition than a nocturne. A beautiful symphony is better than a dull symphonic poem, and vice versa, because the one brings the listener nearer to his catharsis than the other. A fugue and a nocturne both appeal to the listener's feelings through his understanding. The fugue may become so entangled in the understanding that it gets no further, just as the nocturne may be so sentimental that the understanding can find nothing in it to grip, and then the problem for discussion is whether we can postulate any ratio between the two appeals, or fix any limits to the importance either must assume. There *are* more or less beautiful symphonies and fugues and nocturnes, and opinion, experienced and educated, does 'tend to a common focus' in judging specimens of each class of composition. But in trying to compare one class with another we enter an arena where the dogmatic assertion of personal preference is the only weapon with which either side can fight.

I will now try to sum up briefly the position that I have tried to reach, and from which I mean to argue in the remaining lectures, by giving what seem to me the answers to the three questions we ask about art as about everything else: What, How, and Why.

What is art?

To the artist it is a presentation in form of feeling which he has experienced. In its highest aspect it is a presentation of his own catharsis, though a great deal that we would not willingly lose has its origin in feeling on a lower plane. But it must originate in *some* feeling, or it is manufacture from the artist's point of view, even if it deceives the whole world.

'Presentation in form' means that the artist, having felt, can express that feeling in words, colour, or sound, and his deftness in doing so is called 'technique'. Many human beings can express their feeling in some medium so that it can subsequently remind them successfully of the feeling that created it; some can express it so that you and I can understand what the artist felt; but only the great artist can succeed in making you and me experience the feeling that, in him, created the work of art. The object of the work of art—though the artist himself may have had no object but the satisfaction of his own impulse to create—is to communicate to us this reflection of the artist's feeling, a reflection which is often called, somewhat loosely, ' substituted emotion '.

How does art make this contact between two minds ?

Our reaction to certain sensations is accompanied by a feeling of pleasure. The artist works on the discovery that the sensations of sound and colour can be so arranged that the understanding can grasp the arrangement, and that then the feeling of pleasure can be indefinitely intensified. We know that the part you understand is not art : that if we feel pleasure when he says, ' fast falls the eventide ', the pleasure is in no way due to the fact that it is getting dark ; but we know also that if we did not understand the meaning of what he says the pleasure would not arise, because the road through the understanding would be blocked. Were we to say, like children, that we enjoyed the sound of the sentence even though it meant nothing to us, then we are abandoning our claim to enjoy it as poetry, and our pleasure is in a rhythmical arrangement of sound, which is music. The part played by the understanding in enjoying music will be dealt with in later lectures, when I shall recur to the indispensable necessity of structure. But if you grant the fact that the understanding is an essential channel to be passed through, on its way to your feelings, by every artistic appeal, you will confirm my original contention that the more you understand about art the greater will be your enjoyment of it.

What is the final end of art ?

Man has, as the philosophers tell us, a fourfold nature. He has a physical, a moral, an intellectual, and an emotional side. And, as regards the first three of these sides, it is universally recognized as unwise for a man to develop any one to the neglect of the other two. We all lament the earnest and round-shouldered student who dislikes and avoids physical exercise, the keen sportsman who leaves religion to his female relations, the burning moralist who has lost all touch and most sympathy with average humanity. But there seems to be complete indifference, at all events in England, as much amongst professed 'educationists' as amongst the general public, whether the emotional side of a man is developed in any way at all. The one and only conviction an Englishman has about emotion is that you should learn, as early as possible, to suppress it entirely.

Yet this side of man is in reality, as any psychologist will tell you, the most important of the four, since the other three are all, as mathematicians would say, 'functions' of it. To suppress it is impossible, and repression—the only substitute for suppression—is doubly dangerous, for it means that no attempt is made at guiding emotion into the right channels, and also that, although we think we have our heel on it, it is insidiously working its will within us and controlling our every action, and instead of being our most valuable servant, it becomes an invisible tyrant. What exercise should be to the physical side of our lives, religion to our moral, and learning to our intellectual side, this can art be, and nothing else but art, to our emotional side. A man may be physically perfect, stainlessly upright, and intellectually the envy of his friends, but if his emotional nature is closed to the refreshment, the strengthening, and the stimulation of art, he will come to the grave with no inkling of what life can mean when tasted to the full.

IV

WHAT IS MUSICAL CRITICISM?

In the first lecture I spoke to you about the raw material—sound—which alone makes music possible. In the second I tried to outline how human beings gradually awoke to the potentialities of this material, how little by little they found out the various modes in which they could make use of it, and how, finally, combining these modes together, they attained, after countless centuries of experiment, the moment when modern music was born. In the third lecture I spoke of the reactions of ourselves, as listeners, to the works of art which the creative minds presented to us. The three lectures were, if I may describe them in grandiloquent terms, physical, historical, and psychological. In the next three I shall turn to the critical aspect of music, and try to put before you the basis of discrimination, inquiring how we are to tell good from bad, and more especially how we are to increase our enjoyment of music by making sure of not missing what is good.

After my last lecture I am hoping that you will allow the part played by the understanding in listening to music. You will at all events grant that everybody, however crudely, does discriminate; and you will grant that there is music which a young child or an untutored yokel cannot enjoy as much as you do because, at present, his mental development cannot grasp it. And you will most probably admit—as I do readily myself—that at one time you liked music you now loathe, and that now you like certain things for which at one time you were 'not ready'. Lastly, you will perhaps confess—as I do again—that even now, however earnest you may be in your passion for what is good, you are liable occasionally to be 'taken in'. No one but an insufferably conceited man could refuse all of the admissions I have asked for, and to confess to any of them is to allow that your critical apparatus has not reached that state of perfection where a review of it is entirely superfluous.

Negative definitions, as we all know, lead nowhere. But I am going to begin with two, because they clear so much ground and disperse so many popular misconceptions.

First, *criticism is not finding fault*. Unfortunately the adjective 'critical', as used in everyday conversation, does carry that meaning alone. If a performer is unwilling to do a thing before you at which he thinks you are in any way expert, that is the adjective he invariably applies. 'I should not like to play to Paderewski, he would be so critical.' And they picture him to themselves as a Beckmesser waiting hungrily to pounce on every slip. But they are wrong. The best critic is the person who can find beauty where others have missed it. He will teach you to understand and love things which before were outside the pale of your understanding. Where he finds charlatanry he may expose it, and expose it witheringly; but he does not like finding it, and will generally leave it to die alone; and in any case we should hardly call his action 'finding fault'. I assure you, that though I do not know M. Paderewski at all, I would much rather play to him, unpardonable pianist that I am, than risk the ordeal of playing to any music-teacher in Scotland.

Secondly, *criticism is not the statement of personal preference*. When you say, 'I can't stand our Vicar's sermons', you have not made a remark in any way critical, you have merely stated a fact. The only effect your remark can have upon my opinion of the Vicar will be due to my critical opinion of you. I may think you are perverse, or dull-witted, or irreligious, or lacking in concentration ; I may even know that you are deaf. But if you add, ' He is so long-winded ', then the remark is critical, for you have given me a clue to the basis of your judgement, although, if I know you to be a restive person, you have not yet destroyed my sympathy with the Vicar. When a man says, ' I hate Beethoven's symphonies ', he is not venturing into criticism, he is ' letting off steam ' ; though, if he says it often enough, shallow people may

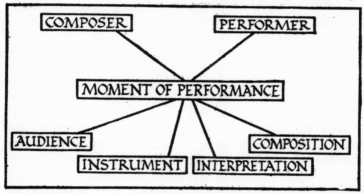

tell him not to be so ' critical '. But when a man says, as one said recently to me, ' After hearing modern music I always feel that Beethoven was trying to say something for which the words hadn't been invented ', then we have a critical remark which might furnish discussion for a happy evening.

Turning from negative to positive, the first necessity of criticism is that you should be clear about what part of the whole you are referring to. Consider what happens in an ordinary case. A composer writes a piece for the piano. A performer comes across it and decides to play it at a concert. At the moment of performance there are four distinct elements: the audience, the instrument, the interpretation, the composition.

Each of these four elements will have its effect on any verdict you pronounce, critical or otherwise. And if you wish your opinion to be well founded it is essential you should be clear in your mind about their relative influences on you.

1. *The audience* may seem negligible as a factor in criticism; but apart from its influence on the artist, who will invariably tell you that his sensitiveness to it supremely affects the standard of his performance, you yourself as a member of an audience are a different man, with different standards of judgement, from the calm and collected person who sits at home in your study. The crowd-feeling is an influence none of us can escape, for no one in a crowd is ever completely ' insulated '. In its exaggerated form you see it in an audience of enthusiastic schoolgirls, to whom the performances of their fellow-pupils all seem flawless. But can you say honestly that you have never over-rated the performance of some one you liked, nor detracted more than was necessary from that of one unpleasant to you? Has your judgement always remained calmly critical when you were one of an audience deeply moved by sympathy, patriotism, or religion? Few of us are so austere, and few would want to be; so that the audience-bias is not quite so negligible as at first sight it seems to be.

2. *The instrument,* by which I mean whatever produces the vibrations which finally reach your ear (whether piano, violin, voice, chorus, orchestra, or what not), is responsible for all the sensuous elements in a performance. The actual tone-quality of what you hear depends, with one slight though important qualification, on the nature of the vibrations produced by some mechanism or mechanisms in action. The qualification is the modification of these vibrations before they reach you, by the building in which you sit; and the importance lies in the fact that we are

all liable to attribute to the sound-producer qualities which belong to the room. How often have you heard it said that some one's voice is ' resonant '? Yet the amount of resonance in the finest voice is negligible compared to the resonance of the room in which you listen to it. And we should be able to adjudge how far the acoustic conditions are, in a given case, helping or hindering the tone. For, as you know, many buildings are bad for sound, some are good ; and the same instrument which sounds to us full and resonant in one hall, will sound thin and colourless in another. Manifestly we should be able, if our verdict is to be true, to estimate roughly the extent of this disability, and ought not unthinkingly to burden the performer with the faults of the building.

Apart from this qualification, however, the instrument is always of an importance which is easily underestimated, more especially when, as is nowadays the rule rather than the exception, ' atmosphere ' is an essential element in the music. I often look back with a feeling of humiliation to an experience of my own. Years ago, when the music of Debussy was almost unknown in England, I heard a pianist play ' La Cathédrale Engloutie ', which I had not heard before. I listened carefully and expectantly, and certainly without any bias against it. I saw at once it was meant to be ' atmospheric ', though I did not know its ' story ' ; and though I knew I must hear it several times again before ' summing up ', yet I felt convinced it was a failure. A few days afterwards I happened to play on the piano which had been used for this performance, and found it to be so worn and ' tinny ' that I could not imagine how the pianist had produced a tone as good as she had done. Given a ' velvety ' piano, I will now listen to that same piece with intense pleasure as often as you will play it to me. I had in my haste been ready, as you see, to condemn a performer and a composition, both of them of the highest class, through my ignorance of the limitations imposed on them by the instrument.

3. *The interpretation* is also an element that you must learn to separate and estimate as a thing apart. Two outstanding facts about it you should know and always bear in mind.

First, we are all of us, quite rightly, sensitive and susceptible to fine interpretation. The performer is there to establish connexion with us by means of his interpretation. The real artist, of course, uses that connexion established between him and you for the purpose of bringing the music to your heart, whilst the charlatan uses it to extort from you admiration of himself; but in both cases the connexion is established only by the interpretation.

The danger to all of us lies in the fact that admiration of and wonder at something immediately and objectively present before us is so much easier and more insinuating than the sustained critical consideration of the matter presented. This truism is a godsend to those who exploit you commercially. A fine singer is paid by a publisher to sing you a tawdry song solely because the publisher knows the interpretation of it will blind your critical powers, and your heartstrings will be so touched that next day you will go and buy a copy. When you sing the same song to your friends you will be disappointed at the effect, and if you are wise you realize that what you thought to be excellence in the song was really skill in interpretation. But there are, apparently, enough unwise listeners still in the world to make it worth while for publishers to go on fooling them.

Secondly, what is the chief quality of good interpretation? I put it to you as performers no less than as listeners. If you have to play the piano to people, to sing to them, to make a speech or preach a sermon to them, there is one overwhelming necessity which makes all other things merely subsidiary, and it is curious how few people seem fully alive to its importance. Recently I had to distribute certificates to a large number of successful candidates in a musical examination, and I asked them the same question. ' When you play the piano or violin, or sing to people, there is one object to aim at so important that the other things, however important they may be when you practise, don't really matter. What is it ? ' And with one accord they answered, ' Not to play wrong notes '. They seemed rather taken aback when I told them they were quite mistaken, and that the aim was to be interesting.

Correctness and conscientiousness and patience and many other things are essentials for any one who wishes to be an artist, but they are essentials of the practice-room and not of the platform. On the platform the supreme consideration is that you should not be dull. You can imagine a sermon which, when read, would be a model of literary grace, of moral insight, and of human sympathy. Yet the preacher of it might send you to sleep by the mere dullness of his delivery ; that is, by his interpretation. And you could equally well imagine a preacher whose sentences scarcely parsed and whose theology did not hang together, who nevertheless could magnetize a congregation for an hour. Consequently, in estimating the value of an interpretation, however much notice you may give, if you are qualified to give it, to the technical equipment of the performer, always ask yourself, first and foremost, whether your attention was held, whether you were really interested, whether you would honestly like to hear it again.

4. *The composition* itself is the only factor in a performance remaining when the other three have been dismissed. Criticism of a piece of music *qua*

composition does not, you will grant, come with good grace from those who know nothing of the technique of composing. But if you bear in mind that ignorance of technique only disqualifies you from finding fault or expressing approval on technical points, and that your judgement on the effect of a work may be sounder than that of a technician, you may feel less inclined to let your modesty belittle the value of your opinion. Of all the people I know in the world the one whose criticism of a new work I should value the most has no conception of what is meant by ' false relation '.

There are four points in a composition which I may loosely call ' intrinsic ', and four ' extrinsic ' (though both terms are inexact), and a consideration of them may help to clear your minds.

Of intrinsic qualities there is (*a*) *Grammar*. It might be more correct to say there used to be grammar. Of the actual ' spelling ' of music you need know nothing. It is, anyhow, a workshop matter, and has no right or wrong except in its effect when it comes to performance. An essay of Stevenson will not please you the less because he spelt some of the words wrong. There is a famous picture of the twelve apostles, which, if you are fond of pictures, you might enjoy. I cannot imagine your enjoyment of it, *qua* picture, would be seriously imperilled if I told you some statistician had discovered there were only twenty-three legs. If some purist maintains that his enjoyment *would* be diminished, and then learnt that there was a tradition that one of the apostles was a one-legged man, I suppose his pleasure would be restored ; proving that the variation of his enjoyment was an intellectual process in the purist and had nothing to do with the merits of the picture.

(*b*) *Conformity to convention*. If a piece of music begins in one key and ends in another, and you do not like the effect, you are entitled to say so ; if the second subject is in the same key as the first (as in the *Meistersinger* Overture) and the monotony of key wearies you, you are also entitled to say so. But the wise man will always refrain from dogmatism, wondering whether the fault may not lie in himself for making a preconceived demand, and remembering that convention, useful as it is as a focus of temporary opinion, is often the stumbling-block of progress.

Then there is (*c*) *the idea*. You are quite as competent to say whether you like the subject-matter of any piece of music as whether you like the ' story ' of a novel. And when you once realize that with experience your valuation of anything changes, you will not be too anxious to attain a sudden power of exact judgement. When you have seen a great deal of football you acquire a discrimination which you cannot possess when you first see the game, and you enjoy it more because you understand it better. Also, you will find a great deal of your understanding has been due to the explanation of the points in the game by those who had reached a more advanced critical stage than yourself.

Exactly the same is true of music. At first you will like it largely because by nature you are susceptible to sound. You will like certain tunes or subjects, and will probably be content, with a certain complacency, that ' you know what you like '. But before long you will find that you tire of the cruder things that pleased you at first, and have begun to appreciate subtler points that had, in the earlier stage, no meaning for you. And then the single condition of your uninterrupted progress to security of judgement is that you should approach things in a receptive spirit, a little humbly, since the composer is at all events likely to know his job better than you and I do, and quite free from that common arrogance which betrays itself in a lightning verdict.

Almost exactly the same remarks apply to (*d*) *the presentation*. When you can discriminate in subject-matter, you will find that the composer's way of presenting it to you is founded on principles and is not haphazard. And the moment you begin to grasp structure—a moment which real ' listening ' will bring to every one—you are a novitiate in that brotherhood of critical minds to whom the secrets of great music are open.

Of the four aspects I have labelled ' extrinsic ' the first is *the sensuous*. Most of us are apt to be more influenced by certain types of tone than by others. Some will be thrilled by a chord on the trombones, others will shiver deliciously to muted strings. In consequence we are apt to ignore the value of the phrase as music, so long as the tone quality touches us. I know some stern critics who veer to the opposite extreme, and maintain that the value of an idea is its value in short score. Truth, as usual, appears to me to lie between, since the ' placing ' of an idea in its medium, even if we grant the idea to be of primary importance, is clearly one of the composer's tasks, and not every idea is suitable for every medium. As an orchestral opening to the opera the first bars of the prelude to *Lohengrin* are ideally successful; played on the piano they mean just nothing at all.

The second and third aspects, *the intellectual* and *the emotional*, I will take together, because I want to make only one point in regard to them. Granted that all music is an appeal to both the understanding and the feelings, the relative importance of the appeal varies. But if the variation oversteps certain limits, the resulting want of balance means deterioration in musical value. The intellectual appeal may swamp the emotional, and vice versa, and we have slang words like ' highbrow ' and ' sloppy ' to describe the results.

It is sometimes, however, forgotten that the range of legitimate variation is not narrow. There is room for the novel and the essay in literature, and there is room for their analogues in music. The novelist is complimented if you call his work beautiful, but the essayist aims primarily at interesting your understanding. Similarly there is music, even in the 'Forty-eight', in which the emotional appeal is at the minimum, and if we say that, however interesting it may be, we have no use for music with so little emotional appeal, we are merely saying that to us personally the minimum required is greater than that demanded by other people. Bach thought he had preserved the balance by not making the emotional appeal fall below the irreducible point-of-stability, and innumerable people agree with him. If you feel otherwise it may be from want of insight, or from natural disability, and in the case of the admittedly great it is best, for a prolonged period of trial, to suspect ourselves of failure rather than them.

Lastly comes the point of *appropriateness*. Things good in themselves are not always good in the wrong place. A *Punch* cartoon may be a perfect work of art in its own *milieu*, but we do not think of using it as an altar-piece. The soldiers' chorus in *Faust* may be perfect as a song for a regiment to shout in a jubilant operatic situation, but as a voluntary in a cathedral it is unforgivable. I do not know how things are in Scotland, but in England we are suffering from an epidemic of the inappropriate in our church music, so universal that it is almost impossible for a reasonably sensitive musician to sit through a service. Chants, hymn-tunes, anthems, and often voluntaries seem to be expressly chosen so that on Sunday you should be reminded of Saturday night. Much of this music, as of a great deal of other music of which one disapproves, is not bad in itself, but only unfitted for its purpose, and a bad hymn-tune may—one very popular one does—make an excellent waltz. So you should keep distinct in your mind the value of a piece of music in itself, and its value when it is applied to a definite purpose.

I must warn you of two pitfalls. There are some things good in themselves which a given individual is, from something fundamental in his nature, unable to tolerate. The aversion is congenital, just like an aversion to tomatoes or venison. We all suffer from some such limitations, and if we are wise—or even fair-minded—we will recognize the limitation as our own and not abuse the cause. Personally, for instance, I cannot read Dickens nor listen to Weber; so I leave them alone, quite genuinely regretting my disability and envying others who can get a pleasure closed to me. The other pitfall arises from association. Certain music works on our feelings through the memories it awakens, and in these cases we should not ' stick up ' for the music, but recognize that our delight in it is entirely non-musical, and that the only part the music plays in the experience is that it acts as the stimulus to our memories. One of the worst hymn-tunes ever written awakens the tenderest memories of my childhood, and a critical attitude towards it is for me impossible. But I avoid it when I can, I keep it out of my own family circle, and I feel a perpetual sense of shame that such a stimulus should work on me.

It is often said that talking about art is a waste of time. So it will always be, unless the talking leads to a change of attitude in the talkers. But I think the attitude of most people to music, even now, is so elementary that it is worth while trying to make them conscious of it. How many people could you trust to find out that a poorly played piece of music was nevertheless a fine composition, or that a finely

sung song was shallow music? I have been trying
to help you to think and talk over the elementary
facts underlying criticism in the knowledge that if
you do you cannot help but improve your discrimination or taste. And if you think, as so many people
apparently do think, that taste is a side-issue of little
importance in practical life, let me recall to you the
words of Ruskin. Some one had twitted him on the
fact that, whatever the subject he was talking on, even
when it was taste, he always ultimately brought it
round to morality. What possible connexion was there
between morality and taste? ' Morality ', he replied,
' *is* taste. Tell me what you like and I will tell you the
kind of man you are.' And with the last sentence
I imagine every psychologist will agree.

V

THE MEANING OF APPRECIATION

You will have noticed that in my previous lectures I have been at pains to make certain words, which we use loosely in conversation, carry a more definite meaning, believing as I do that shallow thinking is more often due to vagueness of terms than to incapacity of mind. I have tried to make you see that a critical mind is not one that adopts a rather querulous and censorious attitude to everything presented to it, but that true criticism is, in the words of a recent writer, a hunt for buried treasure. And I have tried to show that the discriminating mind is not necessarily one provided with the most exact apparatus for classifying things, but that taste is the result of thought guiding feeling.

I now ask you to consider whether you really give the right meaning to the word appreciation, and I will begin by discussing imagination.

If a man is of a certain type of mind, if he is generally dreamy and unpractical, we are apt to label him imaginative. It does not much matter, so long as we understand one another, that we use words loosely in daily life. But when we are definitely inquiring into a branch of life where imagination assumes importance, it becomes imperative that the connotation of the word should be definite. And if you possess imagination, there are two types of it, either of which may be yours; but the two are so distinct, and in some ways so much in opposition, that I think no one can possess both in any full measure.

Imagination may be receptive or creative. If your type is receptive you will ' follow ' quickly. If I tell you the story of a railway accident you will see 'in your mind's eye' the sudden catastrophe, the over-turned carriages, and all the attendant confusion. You will probably even imagine the spot and the surrounding country so vividly that, if you are taken to the scene of the accident, you will say, 'I hadn't thought of it as a bit like that'. For the receptive imagination is primarily reconstructive, and deals with things that are concrete and particular ; it is objective, and works by mental images.

All of us have this form of imagination in some degree, and most of us when young have it in a high state of perfection. Most children actually form mental images of the lions and tigers of the story-teller. All of us, however, listen with less concentration as we grow older, and the power of reconstruction dwindles from atrophy. You should all strive to keep it alive and develop it, in yourselves and especially in your children, for the value to you of any speech, any book, any piece of music depends on your power of holding it in your mind by giving it your con-centrated attention. If one of my children is so absorbed in a book that he does not hear what I say to him, then I am delighted, for that is the way in which a book should be read ; but I think a good many less sophisticated parents would be annoyed and blame the child.

Creative imagination is definitely constructive ; it deals with general and abstract ideas and is subjective. It works through technique, because without the power of presentation in some medium the artist's idea remains for ever in his head. The early stages of everybody's artistic attempts are due to his receptive imagination. If you or I try for the first time to draw a man or write a tune we have to rely on our memory of men and tunes, and will really only be reproducing. But if either of us is endowed with the

creative imagination, our pictures and our compositions will leave the ruts and gradually acquire
a distinction, an ' originality ', which is due solely to
our constructive as distinct from reconstructive powers.
Consequently the more creative imagination we have
the less we use the receptive, and indeed there is
a danger of our losing it entirely.   Few great creative
artists have been good admirers of other people's
work.

Now for appreciation.   I will take for my text the
remark made to me by a man to whom I was maintaining that mind had a part to play in enjoyment.
He replied, ' If I could appreciate anything as much
as a dog does a bone, I should be happy '.   The question of ' as much as ' I shall deal with in my next
lecture, and so will leave alone now.   At the moment
I want to claim that the various forms of appreciation
can be graded, and that it is reasonable to say that one
end of the scale is a lower type, qualitatively, than the
other.   Lecture VI will discuss the quantitative side.

Appreciation falls into three main groups.   They are
not, of course, water-tight, for there is every conceivable step in a range which is continuous.   But the
three types will serve as landmarks.

   1.   *Crude Appreciation* is when we are concerned
with almost pure sensation.   The cat finds the sensation of warmth, when she sits by the fire, to be pleasant,
and memory will suggest her making a habit of it.
The child is pleased with the sound of the trumpet
and wants the sensation to be repeated.   But every
experience in this opening stage is a result of simple
sensation, and ' liking ' is a more appropriate term
than ' appreciating '.   If the latter word is to have
any distinctive connotation to separate it from ' liking '
it must be through the addition of the intellectual
process of comparison and appraisement.   If I have

only once in my life tasted an apple I may like it or dislike it, but I cannot 'appreciate' it *qua* apple unless I have an apple-standard in my mind for comparison; though I may appreciate it *qua* food, if I find it nicer than other kinds of food. So I think it is not a quibble to say that the first time the cat sits by the fire she 'likes' the warmth, and later on may or may not appreciate the experience according as she does, or does not, compare it with other experiences. Appreciation only begins when she says to herself, 'This is a nicer fire than usual' or 'This is better than being outside'.

2. *Intelligent Appreciation* is established when the rudimentary intelligence hitherto scarcely brought into play has become the cardinal feature in the experience, as when a child listens to a story. It won't even 'like' the story if it does not understand what happens; but having understood, it will compare the story with others, and its appreciation depends on its judgement. If you remember I am leaving aside entirely, for the moment, the comparison of the various *quantities* of enjoyment—the cat may, for all I know, enjoy the fire more than the child enjoys the story—I think you will admit that we may claim this 'intelligent appreciation' to be of a 'higher' type than crude appreciation, and that the steps by which the one merges into the other are steps upward. They certainly seem to follow the laws of evolutionary progress, for they develop in an unbroken line, and always in the same direction as we grow from the simple sensational infant to the developed intellectual adult. And if you will admit that these steps are steps upward, and that 'intelligent' is a higher form of appreciation than crude, you are admitting that the controlling factor, the element in appreciation that makes one form better than another, is judgement.

3. Given, then, that we wish to increase our powers of appreciation, as distinct from the quantity of our enjoyment, we must set out to improve our powers of judgement and discrimination. And if we develop these to their limit we attain the third and final stage, the goal of all serious art-lovers, *Critical Appreciation*.

I think that all questions of this kind are made difficult for us because the circumstances of their discussion nearly always arouse the suspicion that some one is trying to 'improve' us. However much we desire improvement in our inner soul, we resent the man who volunteers to undertake the job. So take a case, for your comfort, where you yourself are 'top dog', and I think you will allow that the truth of what I have argued is obvious. Supposing some one told you that your errand boy, aged nine, appreciated as much as you do *Paradise Lost*, or the 'Forty-eight', or some such miraculous testimony to the greatness of man. You resent, and this time quite rightly, the suggestion that mysteries which are only beginning to raise their veil for you, who have spent a lifetime at their shrine, are an open book to a child who has not lived long enough to have formed a standard of anything. He may enjoy the noble sounds, the rolling rhythms, the feeling of splendour and pageantry they evoke, and his enjoyment may be as great as you like; but as to appreciation, that, you will maintain, is not a gift of the senses but a reward of the mind.

True appreciation, then, is no isolated elementary thing, but a nexus. It is feeling combined with understanding, it is our verdict when the appeal to our feelings has been modified by our realization of value, it is 'liking' corrected by judgement.

Should any one deny that 'valuation' is a factor in appreciation, we come, of course, to a standstill.

We use language in a different way. If he seriously maintains that a pig can appreciate port wine, we can only ask him what word he uses to express the fact that to a man one port is better than another. Once he admits the validity of the claim that ' appraisement ' is essential, he must allow the importance of the quality of judgement involved in valuation. It is not, as I explained when speaking *de gustibus*, a question of whether we can say the opinion of Mr. Jones on a glass of port is better than that of Mr. Brown, but whether the opinion of either of these gentlemen becomes more valuable as their judgement becomes riper by experience. So we come back to my original postulate that the better the understanding the greater the appreciation.

The corollary is simple. Improvement in taste means education in understanding. If you want your children to grow up to love great literature you must see to it that they acquire right standards of judgement. They may be by nature sensitive, even over-sensitive, to the emotional appeal of pictures or music or books, and they can only acquire discrimination by the education of their judgement. If we undertake the education our task lies in raising them from the mire of crude appreciation which is the common starting-point for all of us, and leaving them as near as we can to the goal where the power of critical appreciation makes life an inexhaustible well of joy. It is a road every one can travel, and all of us do travel some distance along it ; for even the appreciation of a tale or a tune involves a rudimentary form of ' intelligent appreciation '. Only a fool will ever think the end of the road has been reached, for there is no end, and only conceit will allow any one to think he has gone as far as he might have gone. And the going a little farther, which is possible to all of us, will not only result in an increase of our own enjoyment of life, but will also prevent that atrophy of our power of enjoyment which, as Darwin so pathetically lamented, may make our later years emotionless and grey.

Hitherto, as you will have noticed, I have assumed in pleading the importance of the intellectual side in art that I was addressing people who wished to deny it. In general, especially when talking with young painters or poets or musicians, that assumption is necessary. But the danger that most people ignore or at all events never apprehend this truth, is scarcely greater than the converse danger that those earnest folk who have once realized it carry it to an extreme that defeats its purpose. There is some Puck-like gargoyle in the structure of the human mind that delights, when once it finds us taking a thing seriously, in making us suspect that any deviation from solemnity smacks of flippancy. We acquiesce in our sermons being long and austere, our leading articles being pompous and verbose, our art being pretentious and above our heads, until the acquiescence, if we are too intensely serious, becomes a demand. We like our medicines to be nasty.

There is more than a little danger, in this age of specialization, of those who take music seriously falling into this heresy and preaching the over-intellectualization of their art until the red blood has gone out of it. They forget that the appeal of music is to the feelings, and only to the feelings, and that the one function of the understanding is to act as the link, because there is no other possible link in existence. The intellectual factors in a work of art are only merits in so far as they are facilities in bridging the gulf to the feelings. The cleverness of a fugue, the structural complexity of a symphony, the masked unity of a set of variations, are only justifiable in so far as they help to establish the emotional connexion. It is true that we must not place the standard of intelligence on which the composer may count too low; it has been my main object to insist on our duty of educating this intelligence-link to its utmost limit. But it is equally true that it is easy and common to look on intellectualism in art as an end in itself. If you discuss a theatrical performance with an actor, a picture with an artist, a concert with a musician, another man's poem with a poet, I think you will in most cases be astonished at how much a thing which to you is a matter of feeling, is to them a matter of pure technique. I would remind you of what I said once before: we cannot ' understand ' art, because the part we understand is not art.

There is a *cliché* in common use, amongst people whose talk tends towards ' journalese ', which I should like you to examine and then dismiss from your vocabulary. An artist is often said to ' construct a work of imagination '. At best this is no more than a half-truth. The artist does, it is true, produce his work by the exercise of his creative imagination. His catharsis sets his creative powers to work, almost unconsciously, in that medium in which he has acquired technique. His function in life for you and me, however, is not to construct a work of imagination, but to make us do so. From the purely personal and selfish point of view, of course, the poet's work is ended when his poem is signed, sealed, and delivered. But our concern is with appreciation of the poem, and the function of the poem is to compel us to reconstruct in order that we may feel. It may be so overcharged with the sensuous element as compared with its grip on the understanding—like, for instance, some of Swinburne's poems—that we pronounce it, for our individual selves, a failure. Or it may—like Browning's *Sordello*—put so great a strain on our understanding that we cannot ' reconstruct' anything at all, and our ' feeling' is never called into play. Even the least competent judge of poetry has acquired some standard of judgement, however elementary, to which he will bring the poem for a verdict : a standard acquired from his experience of poems, however limited, which he uses to justify his verdicts even if it is too unorganized to be formulated.

If, then, you would ' appreciate' anything, aim at the enlarging and defining of your standard of judgement. If you think when you listen—or, better still, think after you have listened—you will find inevitably that security of judgement arrives. It has arrived, I should think, to every one in the world in some branch of life. The most unmusical woman here probably feels certain as to the merits of pieces of needlework, and she knows that I, who am now in complete ignorance, would before long attain her certainty of judgement if I devoted time to the study of it. Gradually, but beyond doubt, it would ' come'. The reward is within the reach of every one who desires it, the danger being, indeed, that when it arrives we are apt to feel so self-satisfied that we progress no further. For we must always bear in mind that art is not stagnant, and that we are called on to recast and develop as art changes, recognizing that art is also testing us.

As an antidote to the danger of this self-satisfaction, let me tell you the story of the tourists in the gallery of masterpieces. After ' doing' the gallery in half an hour they disdainfully remarked to the attendant, on leaving, that they did not think very much of his pictures. ' Gentlemen,' replied the attendant, ' these pictures are not here for judgement ; it is the spectators who are on their trial.'

VI

SOME COMMON FALLACIES ABOUT ART

IF you have ever discussed national characteristics with a foreigner you are sure to have been astonished, when the Englishman came up for analysis, at finding it stated as an axiom that with him art counts for nothing. If ever, again, you have tried to start an argument with an Englishman by repeating this, you will be met at once by a whole-hearted denial. The English do, he will tell you, possess a love of art. Leaving aside the truth of the statement that provoked it, I want you to see that the denial is scarcely so convincing as it sounds, even granting its truth.

In the first place, if art is an integral necessity of your life you will love art and not merely the results of it ; for these results often give us a pleasure which, strictly speaking, is non-artistic. The man who loves pictures does not necessarily love the art of painting, and the man who loves a novel is not necessarily fond of literature. And secondly, to like a thing does not make that thing an essential influence in your life. If you are truly imaginative the result is not a mere tendency to occasional dreaminess ; your whole life and character are tinged with imagination. If you are truly religious you do not manifest the fact by your attendance at church, but by every act of your life. Similarly, if you are artistic, the proof does not lie in your 'liking' pictures and music, but in an overwhelming desire for beauty in every cranny of life. It is not a sufficient denial to say you possess a love of art, for the love of art must possess you.

I believe that the lack of desire, in our system of education, to develop the artistic side, is rooted in the widespread misconceptions that exist about what art is and what it can do for us. And in this lecture I am going to tilt at a few of the fallacies most prevalent.

1. *Art is not a decoration.* To most people art seems to be an occasional meal, like afternoon tea, which they take, not because they are hungry or in need of sustenance, but because it happens to be there. Being artistic does not mean possessing the liking and capacity for more of these meals than other folk; it means possessing a frame of mind that demands a relationship between things that will make them at the worst inoffensive and at the best beautiful. A woman does not make a dress beautiful by buying a beautiful material, nor by adding cunning details to it when it has been made. She knows that if it is to be beautiful it must be planned rightly. And all planning and design, that is to say all structure, is the presentation of feeling in terms of understanding. Do you remember the rich ignoramus who brought his artist friend to see the new palace of his own design as it neared completion? 'Isn't it rather ugly?' ventured the friend. 'That will be all right when it's finished,' was the reply; 'they haven't yet put the architecture on.' That embodies a too common view of art, that it is something you can, if you are a little 'precious', add to things, a subsequent and dispensable luxury. Whereas, as I hope you know, it is the only means of communication available to us in those matters that lie beyond language.

2. *Correctness is not an artistic factor.* In some branches of life the main issue is the avoidance of being wrong. In mathematics, for instance, 'a miss is as good as a mile', and in ethics, 'right' is the object aimed at, and attractiveness is looked on with suspicion. But in art correctness is not an end; it is a preliminary condition. In preparation it is, from every point of view, an essential of the first impor-

tance. If I play wrong notes to you, apart from the effect of slovenly work on me (for no one capable of slovenly work is likely to be sensitive in interpretation), I am guilty of rudeness to you and impertinence to the composer. But my performance is not artistic because of its correctness or incorrectness. It is a curious but true instinct that leads us to feel that we are belittling art when we call it ' conscientious '. If some one came on to this platform and recited to you a scene from Shakespeare you might, at the finish, declare it to be ' good ' or ' bad '; it would depend on how far your feelings were reached. If you said ' excellent ', and I then told you the reciter had made twenty mistakes, or if you said ' miserable ', and I told you it was word-perfect, are you then going to say you find you liked it less or more than you had thought?

It is sometimes said that ' Art begins with incorrectness ', and many find it a hard saying. But just suppose that you engaged a dozen fine painters to paint some favourite scene for you. They sit at twelve easels all looking at exactly the same view. If they produce twelve pictures exactly identical they have not produced twelve works of art, but twelve examples of craftsmanship. Art begins when each artist first puts something on his canvas, not because it is there from the photographic or exact point of view, but because it is how he feels, and you will in the end receive, and willingly pay for, twelve widely differing pictures of precisely the same scene. Some of you may have seen a short poem by the late Sir Walter Raleigh, in which this prerogative of the artist is attacked with humorous resentment :

> The artist is a dreadful man :
> He will not do the things he can.
> He does the things he cannot do,
> And we attend the private view.

> The artist uses honest paint
> To represent things as they ain't ;
> He then asks money for the time
> He took to perpetrate the crime.

Sir Walter Raleigh, however, knew quite well—and you would know, when your twelve painters delivered their landscapes—that the ' inexactness ' in an artist's work is not due to lack of the technical skill to reproduce accurately, but to the power of seeing differently. ' When I look at a sunset ', said a lady to Turner, ' I don't see all those colours that you put into it.' ' No, madam,' said the painter, ' but don't you wish you could ? '

3. *Cleverness is not an ingredient of art.* We are apt to think that so long as the pleasure-feeling is aroused it must be artistic excellence that arouses it. To take a crude case, you or I could probably give immense pleasure to a small child by playing, for the first time in our lives, on a 'cello. But the pleasure would derive from the effect of the sound on him, from the novelty, from admiration at our apparent skill, from anything, in fact, but art. As a less crude case consider the intense pleasure you derive, if you are a chess-player, when at length you solve a problem. I have carefully observed, to the best of my ability, the exact type of this feeling-tone that I experience myself. And I am quite certain, unless my introspection is very much at fault, it is exactly the same type that I experience when I apprehend the symmetry in the solution of a contrapuntal problem. I am not saying that the feeling is illegitimate, for art may—and great art continually does—put a tax on the understanding. But the understanding is, as it were, the messenger by whom you communicate with the feelings ; and however wise it may be to interest him in the message in order to ensure delivery and clearness, the messenger himself is clearly subsidiary and his enjoyment a secondary issue.

4. *Art is not concerned solely with the feeling of pleasure.* The unsophisticated person often crystallizes his position, when he comes across a thing he dislikes, in a syllogism that has all the appearance of finality. 'Art deals with beauty : this is ugly : therefore it is not art.' I spoke to you, in an earlier lecture, about ugliness, and put it to you that it is merely a name we give, in art, to things we have not yet learned to use. In music this is, historically, true beyond contradiction. The major third, the common chord, the dominant seventh, have all in their time been considered unbearable. The greatest musicians in the world of a thousand years ago would have thought you dangerously mad if you had played them the ordinary 'full close' with which most compositions now end, and had said it produced in you a feeling of finality. To them it would have been exasperatingly hideous.

Nor is this—the learning to use something called 'ugly' until we see it can be felt as 'beautiful'—the only connexion of ugliness with art. I have often been asked, 'If music aims at beauty, why does it use discords?'

It is a physiological fact that 'relief' gives more pleasure than 'addition'. If, when you are in an ordinary 'normal' state, you get grit in your eye, the intensifying aggravation makes you 'subnormal'. The removal of the grit, which merely raises you to normal, is one of the most exquisite pleasures in the world. To secure the same amount of pleasure, when normal, by means of something positive that would raise you to the supernormal plane, would involve a stimulus out of all correspondence with the grit. Listen to such a chord as this (Ex. 10) in isolation, and you must call it ugly. Yet I think you will change your mind when you find it in the right context, with the relief that its resolution brings (Ex. 11).

Ex. 10   Ex. 11

These two principles, involving the use of what seems ugly, and distressing the mind with the purpose of removing the distress, may be called the principles of context and relief; and in the combination of them lies the justification of discord. If you or I are asked to produce a line of poetry we search our minds, like all tiros, for 'beautiful' words, and conjure up 'amaranth' and 'asphodel'. Not so the great poet. Are there many less promising words in English than 'stuff', 'discontent', and 'sessions'? Yet Shakespeare makes them the nerve-centres in three great lines that you will all remember; for it is the function of a poet to 'raise words to a higher power'. Similarly

Ex. 12

Wagner, *Siegfried*

&c.

Ex. 13

the mind of the inferior composer turns lovingly to 'diminished sevenths' and 'German sixths'. But the great man takes some chord such as Ex. 12, which by itself may sound almost incredibly ugly, and with his magic touch shows you how it may be made to serve his purpose better than all the saccharine chords of the amateur.

5. *Art is not necessarily solemn.* But it is always serious. There are other walks of life in which the confusion of these two words have done untold harm, though in none more than art. It is true that the time has at last arrived when we can speak of a ' great ' work like the *Mikado* without being considered flippant; but it is still unsafe, at all events in England, to speak too openly of the demerits of favourite hymn-tunes. Not that they are solemn—one of the complaints against them is that they seldom are—but that their solemn purpose is supposed to place them on a pedestal where disparagement involves blasphemy. It was Mr. G. K. Chesterton, I think, who once pointed out that any educated man could write a leading article for *The Times*, whilst not one in a thousand could write the front page of *Tit-Bits*. So the writing of a learned eight-part fugue to sacred words, with inhuman solemnity, is within the power of any musician who cares to waste his time learning how to do it; but if he tries to reset the words, ' The sun whose rays are all ablaze ', and then compares his music with Sullivan's, he will have no doubts as to which is the more ' serious ' task.

6. *The appreciation of great art is not the privilege of the initiated.* Mr. McDougall tells us that one of our predominant instincts is ' self-abasement ', though he does not quote, as an illustration, the common suspicion we share that when we like a thing without special training it cannot be very good. It is, once again, the old question of the understanding. Yet the least intellectual of us is capable of appreciating the twenty-third psalm, and I suppose any poet in

F

the world, if he had written that, would willingly sing his *Nunc dimittis*.

It is not necessary for me to traverse again the ground I covered in speaking to you about appreciation. I need only recall the fact that we all can appreciate, though the more elementary our judgement the narrower the field of our enjoyment. If we cultivate our understanding, if (as psychologists would say) we enlarge our ' apperception-masses ', the simplest of us can appreciate an ever-growing number of works of art of the highest calibre.

7. *Criticism is not finding fault.* With this point I dealt at some length in Lecture IV, and need not reopen it. But should you ever talk to your friends or your pupils about the true critical attitude, never tire of impressing on them that the best critic is the one who can discover points of beauty which the others have overlooked.

8. *It is not the whole truth to say that you ' hear' music. You must listen to it.* People often tell me they cannot concentrate in listening, but the statement is not true. Have you ever woken up in the night thinking you heard a sound and then concentrated all the attention at your command listening for a repetition? That is real listening, and it is a thing we can all do with ease. The variation does not occur between the power of different people to do it, but between their abilities to sustain it. And in this, as in every other human activity, the sustaining power increases at every trial. Any one who really wants to may acquire, after a few serious attempts, the power of listening to any composition of normal length, for the attainment is in the main a result of the desire and not of the training. A keen chess-player concentrates on a game lasting for hours, a keen theologian will follow every argument in the longest sermon, a keen card-player can reconstruct

a game for you after it has been played ; but possibly all three will assure you they lack the ability to concentrate their attention on music for even half a minute. They hear it, and may even enjoy hearing it, but the space between their ears acts as a mere sluice-way through which the music flows. There is no concentration, no holding the specimen under the searchlight of the mind. And the true reason is not inability but absence of the keenness which had before been the mainspring of their attention.

9. *The cobbler should not stick to his last.* It would not be difficult to use the above text as the basis for a discussion on education in general, since there is a terrible heresy abroad, with innumerable hosts of ' common sense ' adherents, maintaining (for instance) that if your boy is to be a man of science you must educate him, from the cradle, in science and nothing else. According to this plan, I should, if I wished my son to be a musician, bring him up on music to the exclusion of all education outside the utilitarian minimum that will enable him to add up his pass-book and sign his contracts.

However exaggerated the above may be it does, none the less, epitomize a general attitude that seems to me demonstrably wrong. And it seems to me wrong because of a confusion of ' genius ' with ' ability '. ' Genius ' is in one direction, and the greater the genius of a man the more of a child he notoriously is in other directions. The friends of a poetical genius would feel a little suspicious as to whether he was really the genuine thing if they found he was methodical and accurate over his petty cash.

' Ability ', however, is quite different in kind. A man of ability can turn that ability into any channel he chooses, and will distinguish himself in most of them. Towards some things he will, of course, have a natural bias, and will do best of all in them, and if his bias is very strong, and his ability very great, he may do work in that direction scarcely to be distinguished from the work of a genius. But it is his 'ability' that he has to develop by education, not his ability in some given direction, and if his vocation is to be art, then the greater ability he has developed when the time comes for specialization, the higher will be the value of his output. If you know anything of the lives of men whose names stand out in the history of music you will find no difficulty in believing that if you want to be a great musician you must first see to it that you are a great man.

10. I have kept to the end the fallacy which is, as I think, the most insidious of all. Let us call it the *fallacy of sophistication*. When I was younger, and more inclined to force my opinions about 'good music' down people's throats, the last defence of those reluctant to be converted was always this. 'Day in and day out', they would say, 'we hear a great deal of music and get pleasure, real pleasure, from nine-tenths of it. You want to enlighten me, as you kindly put it, so that I may realize that nine-tenths—possibly the same nine-tenths that I enjoy—is bad. You want, in fact, to divide my pleasure by nine, since you only want me to enjoy one-tenth. I prefer to be unsophisticated.'

Now in my youth I did not know the answer to these folk, and I find that a great many people do not know it now. Yet there *is* an answer, and one of those delightful answers that are convincing, because you can apply it with everybody to some case where they will at once see its truth. Stated as a bare axiom, however, without explanation and application, it does not seem very satisfying, for it is this: that pleasure and enjoyment and delight are things to be measured by quality and not by quantity.

Every one here assuredly understands some one

thing in life thoroughly. I could get you to tell me, if you were arguing against me, of some line in which you had acquired a real power of discrimination. It may be in cigars, port wine, cricket, knitting—anything will do. Now if you really understand batting, would you rather see Hobbs bat for five minutes or see me for an hour? If you really appreciate port, would you rather have one glass of the very best or a larger supply of the ordinary? I have never found it difficult to get an admission of this fact, and to get my opponent to see that quality over-rides quantity. Further, he will generally say frankly that when once discrimination is attained he would rather go without than put up with the inferior. If he cannot get a really good glass of port he would rather have none at all.

My final question in such a case is always this : ' Seeing that your quantity of enjoyment is so reduced by your appreciation of quality, would you willingly go back to the time when you could enjoy the inferior and so have more of it ? ' And it is rather to the credit of the human race that our unanimous answer would, I think, be ' No '. Personally, I would rather never hear another note of music in my life than return to the undiscriminating stage when I liked everything ; I would become a teetotaller at once if I were denied the power of ' appreciating ' wine ; and I think you will all be with me. So should this ' fallacy of sophistication ' tempt any of you to hesitate as to the desirability of making sacrifices in the quantity of your pleasure, think out this argument, apply it to something where the quality of your enjoyment is high, and make the plunge which is a necessary preliminary to all progress in anything under the sun.

VII

THE PLACE OF MUSIC AMONGST THE ARTS

IT is a well-recognized fact that one of the means by which language develops and becomes a more subtle medium for the expression of ideas, lies in the acquisition by words of a 'secondary' meaning. As a simple case, we call a certain material 'wire'; and when it is used for telegraphic purposes we transfer the word to the message sent and say we have received 'a wire'. A little less simply we know the Latin word for sand is 'arena'; the word, then, is transferred to the sand-covered space on which a contest is held, and later we widen its meaning still further and speak of the arena of politics. More complicated still is the use of such a word as touch. At first the act of simple bodily contact, it soon comes to include the feelings: an event is 'touching', an irritable person 'touchy'.

So with the word art. In its primary meaning art applies to action. Everything that we do falls under the heading of art, as all that we know under that of science. The distinction is true to the present day. The science of cookery means the knowledge about cooking that has been accumulated by experience; the art of cookery begins when you light the fire.

When, however, you consider the arts connected with the various senses you will realize that man has discovered that they are not equally tractable. In some cases they have proved capable of organization into systems comprehensible by the intellect, in others no such organization seems possible at present. The former arts, therefore—those that use the eye and the

ear—have been grouped together and given a complimentary name: the Fine Arts. They do not form
a close corporation in any final sense, since there is
no *a priori* reason why the sense of hearing should
have proved a better basis for a fine art than the
sense of smell; and there is no reason in the world
why some genius should not arise to-morrow and show
us how smell can be organized. We pride ourselves
on the fact that our understanding raises us above the
other animals, and so we may perhaps say with reason
that the fine arts, being those in which we have
discovered the means of employing the understanding,
are of a higher type. But if you feel tempted to
preen yourself on your intellectualism I would ask
whether, if you were compelled to choose, you would
prefer to spend the rest of your life amidst good pictures
and good music accompanied by bad cookery and bad
smells, or with the words good and bad transposed.
The answer we should all give may be a little humiliat-
ing to our pride, but it clears the air of pretentiousness.

The process of the artist, as distinct from the function of his art, lies, as I have pointed out to you, in
the presentation of idea in form. If I am a poet,
with the technique of the art at my command, my
experiences and actions are chronological. I feel;
being an artist my immediate consequent impulse is
to create; my creation will embody my feeling,
expressing sadness if I am sad, joy if I am joyful; as
I am a poet I must create in words; as I use words
I must first conceive some idea that can be stated in
language so that it conveys sense; in stating the idea
I must somehow magnetize my words so that they,
and not the sensible idea, carry my feeling. This is
the process of all art. Feeling, impulse, idea, presentation in form—'formal presentation' sometimes
wrongly suggests the idea of 'formality'—in a medium.
As soon as thinkers began to examine Art as a whole

they found, at the outset, a problem that must be solved. The grasp of the whole could only be attained by an examination of the individual arts, and so it was essential to discover some common property in the fine arts which would make comparison between them possible. If no point of contact is possible between architecture and music, then no generalization is possible about art, since art must include both.

This common property, or basis of comparison— what the logicians would call the *fundamentum divisionis*—proved to be the use made of the objective. It became clear that the fine arts—architecture, sculpture, poetry, painting, and music—could be placed in a certain logical order according to the stringency with which they were compelled to refer to the concrete objects of life for their intelligible presentation. It is not a basis involving any disparagement, and there is no justification for assuming that either the first or last in the final order is the highest type. It is a question simply of how far each art is forced to depend on the objective whilst its avowed aim is to be subjective; how far, whilst its purpose is to be presentative, it is compelled by its natural limitations to be representative.

Architecture and sculpture are clearly almost entirely objective. The architect and sculptor produce works which have no meaning unless we can 'refer' them in our minds to some objects with which memory provides us. Place your finger on any square inch of an ordinary statue and you will be touching a 'coat', or a 'leg', or a 'boot', or something which is undeniably objective.

The painter suffers from the same limitations, but in a less aggravated form. He is bound to paint something which is objectively recognizable within limits, but his range is wider and the demand for exactness less stringent. If the sculptor carves a boot it must be a boot and nothing else, for if you are compelled to say 'What a queer sort of boot!' the arresting detail has assumed an importance that destroys the balance. But the painter in his backgrounds, his distances, his mists and sky-effects, is not so tied down to literal accuracy. Both sculptors and painters aim, it is true, at subordinating their 'representativeness' by concentrating the attention, not on the thing represented, but on the part it plays in the form of the statue or picture; holding that truth to art comes before truth to life. Consequently in many great pictures—and in nearly all 'modern' painting—there are many square inches of doubtful nomenclature, though in the main a man is a man and a tree a tree.

In poetry the limitations of the objective are far less stringent. Words are in the main objective, but our minds have been employed, from the cradle, in 'apperceiving' the subjective import of language. So that the poet knows that even purely objective sentences will meet with a subjective interpretation. A tear is an objective thing, but the poet knows that when he exclaims 'Tears, idle tears', you will not concentrate your mind on drops of water running down the cheek, but will subjectively call up the idea of grief.

When we consider music, however, we find that the objective element is non-existent. We can, by simple imitation, recall such things as are connected in our minds with definite sounds. If I were to play a certain interval on the piano you would at once think of a cuckoo. Such possibilities of imitation are the basis of the cruder kind of programme-music, as when the organist, having told you he was going to imitate a storm, puts down as many of the lowest pedals as his boots will cover. But in what is called 'absolute' music—where the basis is the composer's feeling and not his skill in imitation—there is nothing that can be called objective, since 'feeling' is entirely subjective.

I am not arguing *against* programme-music. Indeed, it may be well argued that all music is programme-music in a sense, since it is the conscious embodiment and presentation of something existing antecedent to it. Even the cruder kind may, I think, be forgivable under certain conditions—you will remember the tag about *desipere in loco*, and forgive me confessing I was once extremely amused by a man who could make a harmonium grunt like a pig. I did not look on it as a degradation of music, still less of the harmonium; indeed, I asked him to do it again. But none of you will claim that programme-music in its imitative form, definitely intended to create an objective mental image by its similarity to it, is conceivably the main purpose of the art.

Thus we have the four groups of the fine arts classified with objectivity as the *fundamentum divisionis*. I now want you to consider how we apprehend the content of a work of art in each class.

Architecture, sculpture, and painting exist in space and have no time-reference in them; whereas, at the other end of the scale, poetry and music exist in time and have no space-reference. This three-dimensional quality of architecture is an important factor in our appreciation because our minds instinctively demand stability as a condition in stationary objects. I know of a certain pulpit supported from the ground by one fragile pillar. The knowledge that it would inevitably topple over, preacher and all, unless it were clamped to the wall behind irritates me so much that I cannot attend to the sermon unless I look away from the preacher. Those of you who have read Lessing's *Laocoön* will recognize the principle I am affirming.

Again, stationary things must have a purpose. An

elaborate organ-front, even if you thought it beautiful in itself, becomes pretentious when attached to an American reed organ, and we laugh at its incongruity. Some of you will have seen the beautiful and impressive west front of Wells Cathedral. Yet many people tell me their appreciation of it is marred by the knowledge that it is a mere façade with no purpose, that it is not an integral necessity in the structure, and has really ' nothing to do '.

Painting, like architecture and sculpture, works through our feeling for line, composition, balance, and proportion ; it is three-dimensional also—since the sole purpose of perspective is to create the illusion of a third dimension—and it has the added element of colour. The emotional side of many people responds to it more quickly than to architecture or sculpture, partly because of the additional appeal which the colour makes, partly because the instinctive demand for stability is less insistent. If I saw a picture of the pulpit I might be aware of its bad design as a pulpit and yet enjoy the picture as a picture.

Poetry makes its appeal as ' sense ' clothed in the temporal attributes of sound, rhythm, and rhyme— for rhyme is an attribute involving time, since it demands memory. It is the attributes which make the words ' poetry ', but the words must have ' sense '; which means that some minimum of objectivity must always be present.

I want you here to notice one point. We applied our demand for ' structure ' in architecture and sculpture to the elements of balance and proportion that produce stability. They are properties of the work due to the disposition of the material, and we are applying our minds to purely objective criticism. In painting our criticism remains mainly objective, but also, to a varying extent, it becomes partly subjective because the question of colour occurs, and colour is subjective, whilst bricks and stone are not. In poetry the criticism is also two-sided, for our minds have to 'pass' the more or less objective sentence as a piece of 'sense' before we apply our criticism to it as a piece of poetry. Our criticism of poetry is thus entirely subjective, but is of necessity preceded by an act of objective criticism.

In music the criticism is subjective and nothing else. All relationship with the objective world has ceased, and we have pure sound appealing to us through the channels of melody, harmony, and rhythm. We are still tied down to the one limitation that to reach our feelings there must be the passage through the understanding; but even this passage is made without the taint of any objective element. From the world where material was the only medium we have passed to a world where it is non-existent.

It often happens that musicians, when first they realize this perfection of subjectivity in their craft, assume that it is a kind of spiritual privilege whereby providence endows them with an aesthetic hegemony amongst the fine arts. I do not think this assumption is right. If we were definitely certain that, of architecture and music, one was nobler than the other, I am not at all sure that my vote would be given for music.

But one fact is certain. In the other arts all creators chafe against the objective necessity from which music is free, and they try to be quit of it. Have you ever seen certain sculptures by Rodin—such as those of Balzac and Beethoven—where the attempt is obvious, and in my own valueless opinion quite extraordinarily successful? The normal sculptor would have aimed, by a dignified reproduction of known features, at commemorating a human being. Rodin gives me the impression of genius wrestling with an uncouth material, of mind in a life-and-death struggle with matter ; and you see the dawn of victory. There is a similar example, in case you have never observed it, here in Glasgow on the border of this university. Go and study the statue of Carlyle and see whether, in the light of what I have said, the sculptor was not clearly trying to outspan the limitations of the objective. It may or may not be a good likeness of the ' man ' as a reminder to those who knew him, but as an embodiment of the ' prophet ' to those who never saw him it is both striking and significant.

This endeavour of the less fortunate arts to approach the condition of music has been noticed and analysed by many of the finer critical minds. Such names as Walter Pater, John Addington Symonds, and Sir Henry Hadow will occur to any of you who have read at all widely. But it is sometimes forgotten that the endeavour is *only* towards a nearer approach and not towards the complete elimination of the objective. There is very little of the objective, for instance, in Turner's famous picture of ' Rain, Steam, and Speed ', in the London National Gallery. But there *is* an engine, and there *is* a bridge, and the steam is only intelligible as the objective result of something you know is there. The more subjective these arts become, however, the more forceful seem the arguments of those who maintain that artistic criticism is an impossibility. For their arguments apply only to the subjective side. We can, they admit, discuss the objective side, and say that the sculptor's horse is not much like a horse, or that the painter's lady is ill-proportioned. But that, they add, is not artistic criticism, and we are bound to admit that it is not ; it is the preliminary objective survey we make in order to decide whether the work deserves artistic criticism. Correctness, you will remember, is a preliminary condition and not an ingredient of art : the absence may destroy artistic value but the presence, even at a maximum, cannot create it.

The denial, by these objectors, of the possibility of criticism of the subjective is generally stated in three clear propositions; and while allowing their force we may dispute their finality.

First, they say, there is no language available. Language arises objectively and later subjective inventions are always vague. If I say I saw a cow you know what I mean because we apply the word 'cow' to the same object. If I say I am sad you can only know vaguely what I mean because we can have no certainty that we use the word with the same connotation. It is true, let me grant at once, that the expression of subjective things in language is difficult. But to say it is impossible is to tell every poet that he is wasting his time. It equates the value of the Bible and Bradshaw by making both a mere collection of facts. It implies, carried to its logical extreme, that the whole prolonged endeavour of human beings to make words carry feeling has been in vain, and that we had best revert to the primitive stage where sentences consist of substantives. But to allow that jargon and technical terms are not easy is not to admit that they are useless; for you quickly get to know what a musician means by 'colour' and a painter by 'tone'. And all progress in thinking comes from that 'flash of intuition' with which, as Bergson tells us, we apprehend the relationship or principle underlying some nickname coined to express it.

Secondly, the objection is made, with all the weight of a knock-out blow, that no law of artistic criticism is final. The argument here turns, as you will see at once, on the meaning of the word 'law'. If we leave morality out of the question, for safety's sake, is there any law anywhere which is final? Is it a law that one and one makes two? I should have thought the fact was that when man first added one to one he wanted a name for the new quantity and coined a word. If you say 'But it is always true, so it must be a law', let me remind you of the pragmatic philosopher who pointed out that if you add one drop of water to another you do not get two drops.

I know of no 'laws' of artistic criticism. But I do know that the musical faculty develops both in the history of the human race and in the lifetime of a man ; I know that music 'improves on acquaintance', which means that at first one misses pleasure through lack of understanding; I know that every one has unformulated ideas on 'good' and 'bad' which tend to grow, with experience, into a coherent system of criticism ; and I find that there is a marked unanimity of system amongst those who have thought most, confirming the statement that in all art educated opinion 'tends to a common focus'. If that focus were permanent and stationary then the development of the musical faculty would be an illusion. So that the objection resolves itself, as it seems to me, into a jeremiad that in our attitude towards an ever-changing thing we have not yet learned to stagnate.

Last, we are told that art appeals at once to every one, and so everybody forms his own judgement. This contention is sometimes more tersely expressed by saying that in art the public is the judge. I think I need say little on this point. I have been at pains to convince you that the appreciation of art is not confined to any narrow circle of initiates. Its appeal is the most democratic thing in this world. But you must be an aristocrat in taste, though you may be a tramp in occupation, if you would appreciate to the full. The public *is* the judge, it is true, and on occasion has proved itself a better judge than the specialist. But the undiscriminating public is not the final judge, as every individual member admits when he allows that, in some aspect of life, his own judgement has ripened with knowledge. In matters of art 'it is not people's feeling that is at fault, but their experience'. *Securus judicat orbis* is true, and always will be true, though the world may take many centuries in arriving at the security. But the interval of waiting is not so long as it used to be, and it will tend to disappear with a still greater rapidity when men realize that there is a side of their life which definitely needs the sustenance art has to offer, and that those of them who most persistently ignore the offer are quite possibly those whose need of the sustenance is greatest.

VIII

MELODY

WE are all of us inclined, in our less thoughtful moments, to confuse the functions of analysis and synthesis. If we are of a practical turn of mind we are anxious to see everybody ' doing ', if we are pre-disposed to forethought we strive to restrain folk from precipitate acting ; in both cases forgetting that the two casts of mind, being in opposition, are never present in the same person. The man who does a thing supremely well can never tell you how he does it : the man who can see deeply into the reasons and causes of things is seldom, if ever, endowed with the creative mind.

If you find that, by a gift of nature, you have a good forehand drive, the question of how you do it need never occur, unless you undertake to teach lawn-tennis to some one else; and even then the more natural your drive the more difficult you will find the explanation of it. Indeed, the pupil will probably learn the stroke better and quicker from some one with less natural gift than you for driving, but with a greater power of analysis. And the crucial point is this : that whether the pupil ever learns the stroke from you or not, in analysis lies his only chance of learning how the stroke is done and whether other people are doing it rightly. That is to say, if you are not a born creator, analysis provides your only means of acquiring insight into, and appreciation of, the work of the man who is.

In the light of this fact we can leave the forehand drive and come to melody. It may be that you will never in your life create a fine melody, or even a passable one. It may even be that you do not want to. But you would like, and millions of people would like, to know in what lies the difference between a good tune and a bad one. There is no other way of attaining security of judgement but by the critical comparison of many tunes of all kinds. There are certain elements, such as pitch, accent, &c., which combined together make a melody. The ' mixing ' of the constituents is no way different, in kind, from the mixing of the ingredients of a pudding. The good cook produces something which appeals to you so much that you are a little ashamed of it ; I produce, out of exactly the same material, something you simply cannot eat. Out of the same musical elements I produce a tune you never want to hear again, Mozart produces one that will haunt the world for ever.

Now I might argue, if the point were germane, that analysis improves synthesis. However poor my best tune may be, it will be better if I have earnestly studied great tunes and tried to probe their secrets, than if I work solely by the light of nature ; since in my case nature has already proved an empty quarry. That argument, however, is not my goal, for I want to maintain a different thesis : that though we cannot discover or describe the magic touch that makes certain relationships beautiful, yet we can find, by analysis, that there are certain broad principles followed by melodies we call beautiful and transgressed by those to which we deny the word.

There are four elements in a melody, which I propose to consider in order—rhythm, curve, harmony, and structure.

1. *Rhythm.* In speaking of the ' drum stage ' of music I pointed out how universal and elemental is this appeal. ' In the beginning was Rhythm ', said von Bülow. Our breathing and the beating of our

hearts are periodic, and the baby beats its fist on its pillow in a regular periodicity months before it has learned the elements of pitch. All elementary minds are attracted first and foremost by rhythm, and some of you may remember that Plutarch in describing the meeting of Antony and Cleopatra tells us how the spectators were struck—when there must have been so much else to notice—by the fact that the steps of the dancers kept time to the rhythm of the oars.

Now in this susceptibility to elementary rhythm there lie two great dangers, due to the inertness and laziness which beset all of us. First, as soon as we 'take in' a rhythmical figure we like it so much that, ignoring 'pitch' altogether, we say we like the 'tune'. A plebiscite in England once revealed the fact that the favourite hymn-tune was one that began as follows :

Ex. 14

and I have frequently heard 'The Lost Chord' spoken of as a song with a beautiful melody :

Ex. 15

I am not in any way attempting to disparage these two compositions when I ask you to consider whether they appeal as melodies, or whether it is not the simple element of rhythm that attracts admirers.

Secondly, simple minds like the primary rhythms to be repeated, and repeated as often as possible ; and laziness makes them continue to get their enjoy-

ment from the familiar fount. Albert Chevalier gave
us a proof of this in his immensely popular song,
' Mrs. 'Enry 'Awkins ' .

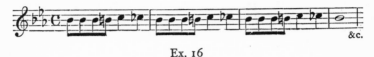

Ex. 16

And Sir Henry Hadow has often quoted another
example sung by everybody in our youth :

Ex. 17

I am not saying that such examples as the above
ought not to attract unsophisticated folk. They
always have done so, and always will. But I ask you
to see that they put the minimum of strain on your
intelligence and that it is mere laziness if we are
content with it. They are like the riddles of children ;
not necessarily bad riddles, but so obvious that they
give our minds nothing to do. And they are pro-
truding one element in a fourfold whole so much
that the other three are entirely obscured.

As soon as the mind acquires the power of grasping
something less elementary than reiteration, it begins
to delight in experiment. First there comes the power
of perceiving ' balance ' amongst little primary rhythms,
and later the demand, just as in poetry, that combinations of primary rhythms shall balance each other
in length. Thus the grip of secondary rhythm, or
bar-rhythm, is consolidated. And when once the mind
feels secure of the normal bar-length of a phrase it
begins to take pleasure in having tricks played on it.

Do not make the mistake of thinking that such 'tricks' are intellectual subtleties which are likely to baffle the unsophisticated listener. Some of the most straightforward melodies—tunes which no one, however determined on abuse, could conceivably call perplexing—have rhythmical schemes of considerable complexity. For instance, most of you will know Schubert's song, 'Who is Sylvia?' though I expect few of you have ever examined its bar-rhythm. Yet this, in spite of its apparent perfect ingenuousness, is so unusual that few composers would like the task of producing a melody on the same framework. Its scheme is

Four-bar phrase, two-bar phrase, one bar :
Four-bar phrase, two-bar phrase, one bar :
Four-bar phrase, four-bar phrase.

Complexity of a different kind, involving unequal rhythms, is exemplified in the two following examples from Tchaikovski, the first (the $\frac{5}{4}$ movement from the Pathetic Symphony) demanding the grasp of alternate two- and three-pulse units, the second (from the string quartet in F minor) making the more elaborate demand that we fuse into one rhythmical whole two two-pulse units followed by one three-pulse :

Ex. 18

Ex. 19

Sometimes, again, the composer will deliberately throw the mind ' out of step' by cross accent, counting on the intensified pleasure we shall feel when our ' puzzled moment' is removed by a return to the normal. A good example occurs in Brahms's *Requiem*, where four bars of three-time are, as it were, decanted into three bars of four-time :

Come   re - joi   -   cing un   - to Zi   - on,

Ex. 2c

It is worth while saying a word on the still more sophisticated question of ' combinations' of rhythm, if only because an understanding of this point is necessary before you can begin to appreciate the music of the Tudor period which is now beginning to come into its own. The composers of that period wrote counterpoint, and we have been taught that counterpoint is the art of combining melodies. As a matter of fact this does not describe Tudor music. The composers then set out to combine rhythms, and left the melodies for the most part to look after themselves.

Fot instance, I recently came across a duet for two trebles in an anthem whose date, at all events, was modern. The final phrase was

Praise the   Lord with   me.

Ex. 21

If any Tudor composer could be imagined to have written so naïve a phrase he would instinctively have tried, somehow or other, to redeem it by making it contrapuntal. And he would have thought of altering the rhythm, in order to do so, rather than the notes. Any two people in this room could sing the above without difficulty. But you will be surprised at the added difficulty of rhythm if you try to sing it as it might have been written in Tudor times (Ex. 22); and I expect you will be surprised also at the curious added interest, when you have mastered it, which the new rhythmical combination gives to it :

Praise the Lord with me.

Praise the Lord with me.

Ex. 22

2. *Curve.* If a single note is reiterated, with or without rhythm, we feel that it is analogous to a straight line. Whether it could be called a melody is one of those purely doctrinaire questions—such as whether two grains of sand make a heap—which would have enthralled medieval logicians and may still be left to the schoolmen. We may call it a ' special form ' of melody, as mathematicians call a straight line a special form of curve. And when this straight line of sound is made definitely melodic by variation of pitch, we feel that the analogy may be extended, and speak of the ' curve ' of melody to describe its movements ' up and down '.

I pointed out to you in an earlier lecture that the first interval discovered with certainty of relationship, both by primitive peoples and by ourselves in our perambulators, is the fourth. That seems to be invariable. A start has to be made with *some* interval, and there are *a priori* scientific reasons, as I explained, why choice should fall on the fourth. There seems to be no unanimity in the next step. There is always the realization that room exists for notes between those constituting a fourth, but infinite divergence in the attempts made to discover them. Sooner or later, of course, the thinker comes along and discovers that if, say, G is the fourth below C, there is also a fourth above, and F is discovered. Having found F and G, though at a distance, the discovery of the whole tone is merely a matter of time. And when the major third E, which as fifth partial has been calling to them unheeded all the time, at last attracts attention then the foundations of the scale are laid.

But experiments in melody do not wait for the discovery of the scale, or even of the tetrachord, for theory follows and does not precede practice. Even your baby tries for variation of pitch before he discovers his fourth; but his extemporizations are not progressions of notes, they are 'swirls'. Melody proper cannot begin until some relationship between two notes, definite and permanent, has been established.

It is clear that when once men had begun making tunes, however rudimentary in type, there would follow (as always follows in everything) an attempt to 'organize'. All evolution is due to this insatiable craving of the mind for system. As a result, various principles of pitch would gradually come to light. It would be found, for instance, just as in speech (and Spencer thought *from* speech) that pitch rose with intensity of feeling, so that the higher note must come at the more emotional point, and the highest note at the climax. That principle still holds good, for it is an everlasting one. When, for example, Mendelssohn has to set the words, ' O God, hear my

cry ', in *Hear my prayer*, he instinctively rises to a
high note on the word ' God ' :

O   God, . . hear my cry.

Ex. 23

And when at the end he forsakes the high note and
writes

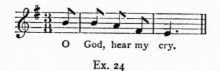

O   God, hear my   cry.

Ex. 24

I think you will feel, as I do, that it is the logical
expression of exhaustion following a crisis.

Again, at an early stage will occur the combination
of melody and words. Not, for a long time, the
' setting ' of words to a tune, but the reverse ; as
when a mother, crooning her child to sleep, will add
chance words to the phrase she reiterates. Before
long will dawn the recognition of analogy, and an
elementary form of word-painting is established. That
also (though often worked to death) is a principle still
holding good. Here is an example you will know :

Lift thine eyes, O   lift thine eyes.

Ex. 25

If Mendelssohn had made the melody fall while the
words suggest rising you would have felt he was being
almost childishly perverse.

A third principle would be the realization that the mind attributed finality to a certain note, and gradually the principle of the ' tonic ' would be established. Later, when it had been found that you could break a sentence by breathing and continue without destroying its unity—the principle of the comma and semicolon in speech—the relative importance of the notes which felt satisfactory at these temporary halts would become established, and the ground is ready both for the subtler developments of bar-rhythm and structure, and also for the embellishment of harmony.

3. *Harmony*. It may seem paradoxical to claim harmony as an element in melody, since by definition melody is sound in one line and harmony sounds in combination. But it must be remembered that, although harmony is historically subsequent to melody, it is not a new invention. The first time a human being heard a sound of definite pitch he also, though unwittingly, heard a chord. And further, usii g the word in the wider sense in which it is now universally used, the principles which underlay all his earliest discoveries in the relationship of notes were harmonic principles. Our knowledge of harmony has come to us from the realization of facts inherent in melodies, and not as the discovery of something we have found we can apply to melody. And though the many beautiful melodies of plainsong and folksong were intended to be sung without harmonic accompaniment, and are indeed far better without it, yet all the features of balance, cadence, and structure which make them finished organisms instead of tentative experiments are due to the harmonic sensitiveness of their creators.

It is said, probably with truth, that we nowadays cannot think of a tune without mentally giving it some form of chordal accompaniment, however vague. I am not convinced that any one ever could. As soon

as the principle of a ' tonic ' was discovered—and
before that moment tunes were mere gropings—the
mind would hold fast to the memory of the key-note;
as soon as it was found that you could get to the
dominant and make a break for breath, the mind,
placing the key-note in the ' margin ' and admitting
the dominant to the ' focus ' of consciousness, would
await the return home. But it seems to me certain
that the dominant was found to be important and
satisfying because its fifth partial was ' major '. If,
that is to say, nature had ordained that the fifth
partial-tone of A was to be C♮ and not C♯, I do not
think the musically-primitive mind would have been
able, when A occurred at the breathing-place, to
retain its hold on D as the key-note.

That is an excursus which will probably appeal to
few of you, but I think you may all be able to see the
implications. The ' punctuation ' of melodies led to,
even if it did not involve at the time, an appreciation
of the relative values of chords (and later of modula-
tions) at particular places. Once the importance of
the key-note as the centre of gravity was established,
the recognition of the key-chord followed ; and the
temporary delegation of its importance to another
chord or key was found to give pleasure by avoiding
monotony of reference. The thing done to avoid
monotony then became an end in itself, as the mind
became more and more capable of retaining the prime-
key whilst exploiting others, and the distribution of
key proved to be, what it still is, the controlling factor
in structure, because without it structure could never
have been developed.

An additional function of harmony, as distinct from
mere accompaniment, arose at a late stage, when
certain notes came to be introduced into melodies
which were only comprehensible in the light of the
chord underlying them. If you know the opening

melody of the first movement of Brahms's Sextet in B flat you will find a note—D flat—of this class. The chord is used, as it were, to give a sudden touch of colour to a tune hitherto a diatonic monochrome. It is like the poppy in a cornfield, and gives us a new focus.

Of structure, or form, I am going to speak in my next lecture, and will end this one by trying to give you the clue to excellence in respect of the three characteristics dealt with here. That clue is balance. If you wish to know a good tune from a bad one, make sure, first of all, that the rhythm, the curve, and the harmonic scheme all have purpose, and that none of them protrudes itself unduly. You will then have reached a stage of criticism where you are free from the cruder errors of judgement, and well on the road to that more subtle security at which we are all aiming. You will know better than to speak highly of a melody when you have really only been caught by its rhythm, just as you now know better than to say an exciting story is, *ipso facto*, a fine piece of literature. For you will know that if the rhythm has been so striking as to obliterate the curve, then the melody lacks essential balance.

You will find, before long, that you have often been searching for melody in the wrong place, falling into that curiously modern error of thinking it is necessarily the ' top line '. That is an error which will keep you for ever from understanding your Bach, and what Mark Pattison said of Milton is even truer of Bach ; for the appreciation of him is a final and sufficient reward for all the labour spent in its attainment.

Last, you will become a connoisseur of claptrap. Just as you will have learnt to judge when a sequence is the padding of facile insincerity and when it is the outcome of cumulating interest or of structural necessity, so you will find you can tell whether the

FLOWERS IN THE VALLEY

Old English Melody

Ex. 26

' high-light ' of an unusual harmony is the true expression of feeling pressed to a point, or is mere stolen honey.

As a specimen of a truly beautiful melody I should like to send you away humming one which may be new to most of you, though it is fairly well known in England. It has always seemed to me to fulfil every demand we could make of a fine tune. Rhythmically it is varied and insinuating without being arresting ; melodically it is almost entirely ' conjunct ', never making a jump without a motive, and its curve is that of a quiet feeling rising and falling, making its top note, once reached, its only climax ; harmonically, it is as simple as a tune can be, yet manages to create the feeling that when we at last reach the final chord we have attained the object of a quest [see Ex. 26, on p. 109].

IX

ON FORM

In talking to you about form, or structure, in music, I am going to make the uncomplimentary assumption that you know absolutely nothing about it—not even the meaning of the word. Almost all the talking about form that I have ever heard has taken it for granted that the listener grasped its nature, admitted its necessity, and only needed to be initiated into the structural mysteries of a Beethoven first-movement. So I will begin by trying to show you that not only in the fine arts, but in all the arts of life—in everything whatever that you do—form is the name we give, not to any aspect or quality of the work, however essential, but to the one supreme governing principle which constitutes its individuality, to which all its aspects and qualities are subservient, since from it they derive.

Take an obvious instance. Think of the dining-room table you have at home, and then look at the table on this platform. Both are tables, the one as much as the other. They may be, this table and yours, identical in every respect—wood, colouring, shape, ornamentation, and measurements the same to a hair's breadth. In this case the difference between them is a metaphysical difference, outside the region of our inquiry. But they will presumably be quite unlike each other, having in common only the bare fact that both are tables.

If you analyse the difference between them you will find that they fall under two headings, qualitative and quantitative. Under the former heading come such things as the accidental attributes of material, purpose, and the like : a mahogany card-table and an oak dining-table differ in this way. With such attributes form is not concerned beyond the *a priori* fact that material and purpose are amongst the factors that govern the maker's choice of form. The essential individuality of a table consists in its shape, that is, in the relation of its parts. If a magician could at a touch transmute a plain deal kitchen-table into rosewood or solid gold he has not changed the ' form ' of the table ; but if a schoolboy with a saw shortens the legs he has succeeded where the magician failed. This table is itself *because* of its form, and if the maker had made it of something else it would still, *qua* table, be the same ; but if he had ' presented ' his idea of a table in different measurements we should have had, not this table, but another.

The case is the same with music. Form is not dependent on material, since two movements may be in identical form with material entirely different. Neither is form an ' aspect ' of a movement, since it is the one condition of existence without which no idea can find its presentation. It is the process of objectification by which the artist, provided with ideas by his creative impulse, co-ordinates his aims and methods, and adjusts them to the final end of presentation, and in the absence of such co-ordination and adjustment his highest endeavours will degenerate into mere meanderings. And it is in this light that I now want to try to prove to you that an examination of form may help us, by substituting discrimination for ingenuousness, to appreciate music the better.

All work, if it is to be done properly, involves preliminary preparation and thought. Consider a humble instance. If I were a guest in your house and asked you to make me a cup of tea, let us suppose you went and made it yourself. There is an art in doing it,

the cup of tea is the ' work of art ', and its excellence
depends on your technique—though you need a
reasonably good tea, just as Paderewski needs a reasonably good piano. But before your technique comes
into operation your mind schemes a plan of action.
You light the fire or stove, put the kettle on, and wait
for the boil ; meanwhile you find teapot, cup, spoons,
and make sure they are clean ; you fetch milk, sugar,
and a tray from where your memory tells you they
are kept. The actual ' making ' of the tea is a small
matter compared with its many preliminaries, yet its
excellence will be spoiled by a dirty cup, sour milk,
or any preparatory negligence.

To the poet the same process is necessary. You
will, I am sure, have grown out of your childish conception of him as a person of sudden frenzied inspira-
tion, sitting down to fill his paper at breakneck speed
whilst the white heat of fever is on him. Think of
him as the calm and critical worker, slow and un-
hurried, that he usually is. He does not produce
a poem and then examine it to see what its characteristics are. He produces an idea, and then—just
as you do in making tea—arranges his preliminaries.
Before he writes a word—probably before his idea
has shaped itself into definite language at all—he has
settled whether he will write a long poem or a lyric,
in blank verse or rhyme, a sonnet or a poem in stanzas,
couplets or quatrains, and has more than a vague idea
of his whole metrical scheme. He knows, in a word,
that his idea must be presented to you on some plan,
and that the plan is precedent to the presentation.

The same is true of the composer. He does not, in
a sudden ecstasy, fill a page with notes and then look
at them in order to discover whether he has written
a funeral march or a waltz. He knows, before he
writes down a note, many facts that he could tell
you. He knows his mood—the original impetus that

made him want to create. He knows that his music, if it truly represents his mood, will be, let us say, wistful and dreamy, though perhaps he has not yet decided whether he will make a nocturne of it or whether it will be sufficiently deep and serious for more epic treatment. He is getting it, in his mind, into definite shape, and will soon tell you its key and time, and whether he thinks it will best suit a solo instrument or an orchestra.

All these preliminary conditions are conditions of form, because they are problems on the solution of which the presentation depends. Thus the form or plan is not, as so many ingenuous folk conceive, an aspect of a thing, it is the condition on which alone the idea can develop into an organism, as the embryo develops into a man. The materials in a builder's yard may be arranged so as to make a house, or several different houses ; but the difference between the houses, the one and only distinction that makes each house individual and distinct from the others, lies in the arrangement of the material, which is to say in its plan, or structure, or form.

Instead of dealing, like most lecturers on form, with movements, I am going to examine a simpler thing, the structure of melody. Suppose that we were now at that stage of musical history where our parents, having discovered the interval of a fourth, had been entirely satisfied with melodies that reiterated it, and that the most advanced melody we had ever heard was

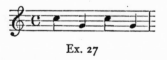

Ex. 27

We, being young and disrespectful, would pain them by saying this sort of thing bored us, and might break all tradition by insisting on developing the idea into

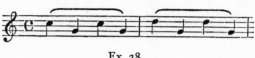

Ex. 28

We should then find that our own children, instead of putting up statues to commemorate our advance, felt bored in their turn by such a small field of interest. They, as we had done, would be asking themselves the eternal question, ' Isn't there something else we can do?' And this process would continue, generation by generation, sometimes forward, sometimes backward, sometimes down a cul-de-sac—though at the time no one would know which, any more than they know in the processes of to-day—and each innovation would assuredly cause just the same shakings of the head as the more stupid of us now indulge in over Ornstein and Stravinski.

In the course of many generations it would be found that the difficulty of composing was no longer the difficulty of doing something different, but of choosing between the many things that could be done. The mind had acquired the power of ' holding' a phrase of some length, so that what had at first been a process of experiments crystallizing into new formulae became a process of deliberate choice or invention, and the artisan became the artist.

Let us now analyse the plan of the melody I played to you at the end of my last lecture—' Flowers in the Valley'. Supposing the first little rhythmical figure, which is the germ of the whole tune, had occurred to you or me—

Ex. 29

What should we have done with it? There are dozens
of replies to the question, 'What shall we do next?'
Here are some of them, all quite reasonable:

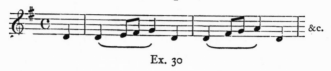

Ex. 30

Ex. 31

Ex. 32

The composer, if it is the work of one man, or the
folk-mind, if it is the result of the friction of use,
knew better. The simplicity and tenableness of the
germ justifies, and almost demands, an extension in
line, and we get the far more beautiful and graceful

Ex. 33

You and I might have continued the phrase again in
many ways. For instance—

Ex. 34

Ex. 35

I wonder if you feel at all sure what are the weaknesses of these two alternatives? In the former the opening rhythmical-figure is too prominent, being insisted on to the point of weariness, and also the top D, which in the real tune is held back for the climax, is here suddenly jumped at in the wrong place and for no reason at all. In the latter these two faults are avoided, but two others introduced. For it is not, melodically, much more than a simple arabesque round the key-note, and also, since Ex. 33 ends on G, the further insistence and repeated cadence on the same note is a confession that in the first case we had unskilfully got there too soon.

The structural instinct that created the original was better than any of our suggestions. It felt the necessity of going somewhere away from G, and having decided that the crucial necessity was a question of pitch it felt also that the moment was inopportune for the introduction of fresh material, so used the opening phrase again :

Ex. 36

Again the question arises what is to be done next. The four-bar phrase is complete; it is not final, since the composer ultimately tells us his ' home-note ' was G ; there is no one and only continuation. The phrase may possibly have been stored for a long time in the mind awaiting the moment when some flash of intuition, or a recurrence of the original feeling-impetus, suggested· a continuation that would seem inevitable.

There is one consideration, of special importance at this point, which has not been recognized as clearly as it deserves.   We all tend to group things in multiples of two.   The elementary form of balance is of one thing with another.   The poet must have concentrated on producing a second line to balance his first long before the more complex idea of three lines as a unit could occur to him.   And having established the two-line unit, or couplet, he would (I speak in ignorance, but cannot imagine it was otherwise) proceed to add, not another line, but another couplet, and so arrive at a four-line unit.   To this day the normal poetry, apart from ·blank verse, is of this type, and if you or I had to produce something called verse, I think we should, beyond doubt, write our nonsense in stanzas of two, four, or eight lines.

In music, even if the above is untrue of poetry, the principle applies.   The feeling for the four-bar phrase is so ingrained in the normal man that it is almost impossible, as Wagner found, to rid him of it.   If any of you ever try to compose, just take a six-line hymn and write a tune for it.   You will soon be convinced of the existence of curious subtleties in the matter of rhythm and key that arise from the intrusion of a triple element into the structure.

If this tendency of our instinct for rhythm is granted, and if it is remembered that the development of periodic rhythm in music is due to the conditions imposed by those activities—dancing, reaping, poetry, &c.—which in themselves arose from that instinct, it seems inevitable that melodies should, normally, be multiples of two.   Ex. 36 is a four-bar phrase, and might well have been completed by a second one.   The composer felt otherwise, and decided on sixteen bars. Possibly he recognized that the quiet restraint of its character would make it insignificant if it were so short as eight bars ; possibly he was actually setting the eight-line stanzas to which the tune is sung.

The composer, then, having four phrases to produce, must have a plan. Four distinct unrelated phrases will not be an organized melody, beginning with an idea and ending when the organism is perfected ; it will be a meaningless meander, ' leaving off ' somewhere merely because it cannot go on for ever. On what plan, then, can he organize it ?

The first generally accepted agreement is that the last section—in this melody bars 13–16—shall be in some way a restatement of the main ideas that formed the material for the composition. The technical name for this is recapitulation or reprise, and it is due to the same instinct that leads a speaker or writer to ' recapitulate ' for your benefit at the end of a discussion.

There are still two four-bar sections to be provided for, and on what plan can this be done ? If both are new there will be three sections of material to be crammed into one section of recapitulation, and the result can hardly be organic. There are many possible plans. You can, for instance, have a new second section and then repeat both, with possibly a modified ending, making the tune of the form 1·2·1·2. Or you might do the same, reversing the last two, making the form 1·2·2·1.

The plan, however, which proved most attractive to the human mind was this. For the second section repeat the first ; for the third ' comment ' on the first, not in any way slavishly reproducing it, but using some germ inherent in it and supplying any deficiencies you think important ; for the last section recapitulate the first with such modifications as you think necessary to produce the effect of finality as opposed to mere leaving off. I think we do not recognize that in what is called sonata-form the 'repeat' is simply a survival of this problem of finding some occupation for the second section in an ordinary melody where four phrases are the norm. Its presence was always said, in my young days, to be due to the anxiety of the composer lest you should forget his 'subjects', and though the point is unimportant, I think the explanation is historically wrong. Anyhow, the repeats, having lost their whole point (which is balance) in an extended movement, are now seen to be unnecessary and are always, I am glad to say, omitted in performance.

You will see that 'Flowers in the Valley' is completed on the plan I have just described. The second group of four bars is an exact repetition of the first. The third section starts by pretending it is going to make play with the notes A, B, C, which ended the opening rise, and then seems to realize that two necessities are paramount: firstly, to disturb the evenness of the rhythm which by now tends to be a little over-complacent, and secondly, by providing some kind of climax—not too striking, since quiet folk do not shout, but enough to show that having reached a note higher than any other it is time to think about going home.

Ex. 37

For the last section an exact recapitulation of the first would anyhow be a little tame, as we have had it twice already. In this case it would also be impossible, as the composer wishes to end on G and not on D. His method is interesting, and is itself an attraction, for he takes the second half of his opening section, which begins and ends on D, and then repeats it a fourth higher, beginning and ending on G:

Ex. 38

You will see the importance of ' plan ' in another light if you consider how it leads to ' economy of material '. You might think, if you had to compose a sixteen-bar tune, that you would have to invent sixteen bars. When you examine ' Flowers in the Valley ', you will see that there are only six bars really new—1, 2, 4, 10, 11, and 12. And this economy becomes even more important when we try to take in a long movement instead of a comparatively short melody. But there is one point of nomenclature I want to explain to you before dealing with extended compositions.

In some melodies, especially short ones which ' hang together ' more by unity of rhythm than by treatment of material, we get an impression that the composer has a definite intention of getting to a certain point and then, the point not being a final resting-place for the mind, of getting home again. Such a tune is ' Barbara Allen ' :

Ex. 39

The idea of ' there and back ' is clearly in his mind, and the form of the tune is nicknamed *Binary*. The process is obviously twofold in its nature; it is like going out to post a letter, since we have got to come home again; and that is the outstanding mental impression of the form of most tunes that employ, at the half-way house, a cadence which cannot be mentally adjusted to the tonic. Such tunes as ' Mr. John Blunt ', ' The Bonnie Banks o' Loch Lomon'', or ' Drink, puppy, drink ', are binary.

Sometimes, however, you will find a tune reached ' home ' at the half-way halt, as in ' All through the night ':

Ex. 40

I think you will admit that your mind apprehends this tune in a different way. There is a feeling of finality at the end of eight bars (that is to say, after hearing the first section twice) that would not be offended if the tune went no farther. The last section—an exact recapitulation—is distinct in the mind from the third, which has kept the mind waiting for it. The tune is, to use a homely comparison, like a sandwich, two similar outsides with something different in the middle. And such tunes are called *Ternary*. Other examples of ternary tunes are ' Drink to me only ', ' The Miller of the Dee ', and ' Flowers in the Valley '.

I would warn you against attaching too great importance to names. The hard-and-fast purist, for instance, will tell you that 'Flowers in the Valley' is not a ternary tune, because its middle point is not a cadence in the tonic key. If any one thinks its plan is more akin to the plan of 'Barbara Allen' (Ex. 38) than to that of Ex. 39, then I fail to understand him; but we can both of us enjoy the melodies and grasp their structure, so we need not quarrel (as the doctrinaires are still quarrelling) about the exact application of the technical terms.

At some future date I feel certain there will be a Cramb Lecturer who will devote his whole ten lectures to the analysis of form. And he will tell you, I feel equally sure, that the larger forms grew out of the smaller. If you really see the form of 'All through the night' you see the exact plan—many of you will have recognized it already—on which the orthodox first movement of the symphony or sonata is built. There is the opening statement of material, now an organism by itself, following some plan made necessary by its increased length; there is the repeat, now discarded since balance is provided in other ways; there is the 'working out' section, keeping in touch with the original material and supplementing the mere statement by adding intellectual comment, more passionate feeling, and more cumulative climax; and finally there is the recapitulation. Similarly the 'sandwich' may be extended by having as many pieces of bread as you choose with something different between each slice, and you have rondo form in embryo.

Some future lecturer, again, will doubtless tell you how with certain composers the form is the main clue to the mood. They will give you no programme and no hint of their emotional experience except what you discern for yourself in their material and their handling of it. Such compositions we call, because of their method, and in nowise because of their date, 'classical';

giving the name ' romantic ' to those works which, though often in the same ' form ', put the mood in the foreground, and frequently, by their title, announce beforehand the emotional programme. A great deal of ' classical ' music is also, of necessity, ' romantic ' up to a point, but as the biography of feeling becomes more and more the main preoccupation of a composer, so will the need and the desire to suffer any voluntary restrictions in presentation become less and less; until in ' dramatic ' music each step is decided, not by the suggestion of the mind, but by the necessity of the situation.

Such considerations I will leave to my successors, and will only draw your attention to one more point. You may have discovered that the longer you go on at anything the more difficult it becomes to end satisfactorily. If you speak a sentence, you can ' leave off ' without concern ; you have done what you set out to do and it is self-sufficient. Make even the shortest of speeches and you will find that a new difficulty has obtruded ; you cannot just ' leave off ', you must ' finish '. So the ' coda ' was invented. It means anything done with the purpose of making the end conclusive. The ' Amen ' at the end of a hymn, the ascription at the end of a sermon, are both codas. Few of you can honestly say that you have never ended a letter with the quite untrue statement that you *must* finish to catch the post. It may comfort your remorse to know that, though the lie was inartistic because it was borrowed, yet the feeling that prompted it was sound. You had planned your letter badly, for you had used all your material, yet could not leave off without a sense of abruptness ; so you extemporized a coda. Without condoning the offence (since I must have committed it myself) I commend the sense of structural necessity which underlay it, and the commendation may also serve as the coda to this lecture.

X

MUSIC AND PSYCHOLOGY

THERE is one particular paradox in life which has always interested me. A smattering of knowledge is universally looked on with contempt, and yet we zealously strive to add to our knowledge in all directions, fully aware that, save in rare instances, a man can know only one subject thoroughly. We are almost all of us ' amateurs ' in every subject but one, yet we feel it our duty to acquire in other subjects the very smattering we despise.

I must protrude the feeling of duty as my excuse for talking to you, amateur as I am, about psychology. But I may plead two justifications. There is the justification of precedent, since no philosopher has ever hesitated to write about art, a subject in which most of them have proved themselves distressingly amateurish. And there is the more practical justification that all students of music now training as teachers are obliged, by Government edict, to ' take ' psychology as part of their training. This edict, however, caused so much astonishment, and so many demands, half-amused and half-indignant, about what conceivable connexion there might be between psychology and music, that I think a musician may state, without presumption, why he thinks it reasonable and good.

Psychology deals with the way in which we react, or ' behave ', when anything affects us. Being a science it begins with the known facts of reflex action —movements of our bodies which are outside the control of our minds—and then surveys the whole field of muscular reaction, reaching the less purely physiological field that embraces instinct, memory, habit, attention, and so on. Finally, it inquires how we, as thinking animals, can and do control native reactions, and opens the door to the subject whose problems most concern all of us—moral conduct. Our question is, where does all or any of this ' connect ' with music ?

You will remember that the life of man is a four-fold life, and that his activities fall into four provinces —physical, intellectual, aesthetic, and moral. Psychology has something to tell us of definite importance in each of these four fields, something which I believe we can learn in no other way, and something which is of real use to all musicians whether they are training as teachers or no. I will tell you some of the things it has taught me, with one preliminary warning. All of what I am going to say will be known already to some of you, nothing will be new to you all ; but if you have ever mastered anything you will know the difference in value between facts that are merely known and facts which are apprehended as parts of a logical system, as due to the working of cause and effect, as links in a chain. The accumulation of facts may make you well-informed, but knowledge and wisdom come from the discovery of principle.

I. The importance of the physical side of life is obvious to any musician. All executive powers are physical. The teacher who pretends to train a hand or a voice without any knowledge of how muscles work is simply a charlatan. A minimum of anatomical knowledge is essential, but even this minimum is of little use unless you know, in addition to *how* they work, the way to make them work better.

Psychology makes you realize that in all muscular action the goal is the elimination of thinking. At first you must think with all your might. A child learning to walk, or a man learning to drive a golf-ball, is using his mind as much and as intensely as a mathematician concentrating on a problem. But the child cannot walk, nor the man drive, until the moment comes when the mind is freed from the necessity of control. When you were learning to ride a bicycle the furrows on your forehead were an index of the employment of your mind. If any one had asked you ' What is three times seventeen ? ' you would have found yourself in the ditch. Now you can ride, and your mind is free, as the control of the muscles has been delegated to a nerve-centre.

Exactly the same process takes place with every detail of finger action, scale playing, arpeggio work— anything which falls under the heading of ' technique'. At first the whole mind, at last no conscious mind-control at all.

Psychology has more to teach us in the matter of acquiring this automatic muscle-action ; that is to say, how to practise. At first we are using muscles not accustomed to use, and the blood, which is the ' petrol ' of muscular action, becomes quickly exhausted. Then we are ' tired ' ; we have done all the work possible for the moment, and have reached ' saturation point '. Thus we know why several short practices are better than one long one. Any child will improve more with ten minutes' practice a day—in all an hour a week—than with two hours every Saturday.

There are many other facts you can learn about the laws of habit, such as the devastating effect of an exception, if you take the trouble to read an ordinary text-book, and no one is qualified to teach until he knows them. For habit is the bedrock condition of all technical efficiency.

II. In the intellectual field the help of psychology is equally great. If you are aiming at improvement in music, either your pupils' or your own, you must have in view something beyond mere increased executive powers. And if you wish to improve the

mind you surely will have more hope of success if
you know how the mind works. The whole realm of
appreciation, which involves appraisement, is a realm
of the understanding. And even in such minor matters
as the elements of music there is room for a great
deal more psychological acumen.

The first law of understanding is that you need
a thread. If I say 2, 4, 6, 8, you all expect me to
say 10, because you have seen the plan. If I say 2, 17,
9, 21, you can't understand what I am after. All
understanding depends on the grasp of some principle
of relationship. Yet hundreds of students come up
to the great schools of music every year, presumably
the pick of the most gifted young musicians in the
country, and scarcely one of them knows, or has ever
been told, that there is any principle underlying key-
and time-signatures. They may know (some of them
do know) that a key-signature of four flats implies
A flat major or F minor, but they know it as one single
isolated fact in their armoury of knowledge, unrelated
to any other fact and derived from no principle
whatever.

Again, the study of attention and interest—even
the superficial study—will cause you to change your
views on an essential factor in both learning and teaching. We all know that concentration is the founda-
tion of progress, and we desire to acquire the ' gift '
and to establish it in our pupils. Psychology analyses
the conditions of its attainment, and only incurably
stupid people can fail, if they study these conditions,
to learn something that will help them. Let me tell
you two truths out of many. The first condition of
attention is interest. We cannot concentrate on
a thing that is uninteresting. But, you will say, many
people do concentrate on a dull thing because they
desire some other end : a prize, an appointment, an
increased salary, or a sense of duty fulfilled. Your

objection is a true one, and is a statement of the facts
with which most people are fully satisfied, without
taking the trouble to draw the staring conclusion.
For it is really useful to know that interest is of two
kinds, immediate and mediate. No attention is possible
without interest, and if we, or our pupils, have no
interest in the task in hand—if, for instance, we do
not find we get any immediate pleasure out of playing
scales—then no concentration is possible unless we
can raise an interest in the ' end ' for which we know
that scales are a necessary preliminary. No normal
person likes the rigours and restrictions of training,
but they become absolutely interesting if we are once
set on winning the race.

To grasp the relation of interest to attention is to
realize, with a little salutary humiliation, at least one
inevitable deduction. Have you never complained,
in your unenlightened days, that a class was inatten-
tive? It is a complaint I shall never again make
myself, for I know that it means one thing and one
thing only : it is a public statement of the fact that
I have failed to interest them, and have been dull.

A little thought will tell you how this question of
' mediate interest ' quickly brings us round, like serious
thought on anything under the sun, to the province
of morality. Few of the things we have got to do in
our lives are *per se* interesting, and if we are going to
do them well we can rely on nothing but moral purpose, which is determination and character in action.
I remember once hearing Bishop Gore say, out of his
immense experience of all kinds of students, that he
thought he could only make one generalization on
education which was true beyond all doubt. It was
this : that great as was the divergency of natural gifts,
the difference between one man's ability and another's
counted for nothing in comparison with the use made
of them. That is the confirmation of the psychological

truth that however difficult the immediate task may prove from lack of congenial interest, it is your determination to reach your goal, and not your natural gift, that is the dominant condition of victory.

There are many other aspects of this intellectual field of life in which psychology offers to clarify your mind. If I were giving you a lecture on elementary psychology I could tell you facts about memory, association, apperception, and the like, and would confess to you how it humiliates me to recall the dark ages when I was complacently ignorant of them. But if what I have already said about attention and interest fails to induce you to go and find out the rest for yourselves, it is not likely that I should succeed by further garrulity.

III. In what I have called the aesthetic side of man I mean to segregate the realm of feeling. I have been trying to maintain, through nine lectures, that art reigns in the kingdom of feeling, and that no question of good or bad in art, no possibility of any standard of appraisement, can arise for us until we have learned to control feeling by judgement. The lectures have been one long exegesis of a psychological text, and the text is this : that since every action we perform is a reaction, and every reaction is due to feeling, the only possibility of ennobling ourselves into something higher than the beasts of the field lies in ' acquired reaction '.

We all know that in every branch of life we begin by liking the wrong things, and only acquire our standards of taste after many readjustments. We see clearly in the case of our neighbours that what they like is not necessarily what they ought to like, and in matters which we ourselves really understand we know that our neighbours would gain in enjoyment if they increased their discrimination. The whole trouble in matters of art is that few of us are modest enough to apply to ourselves what we know to be true of every-body else. As my whole purpose throughout these lectures has been to try to convince you that this cultivation of the aesthetic side of life is to your pleasure and advantage, even if you fail to look on it as a duty, I think I need not weary you with any recapitulation.

IV. On the moral side I will refrain from saying much; it is too easy to be sententious and prosy. Psychology leaves off when morality steps in, for its duty is done. It has prepared the ground, as I have pointed out, on which moral questions are to be debated, and some day even the theologians will awake to the fact. But I think two considerations are worth stating.

Character is a moral question, and art is funda-mentally dependent on character. The work of an artist is a 'projection of personality', in spite of the fact that the phrase has been discredited owing to the insistence on it by those who pretend that art is nothing else. His work must change if his character changes, so that character must be a 'function' of his work. And from the non-creator's standpoint, character is involved no less, for what we appreciate depends on our own character. You will remember the saying of Ruskin which I recalled to you : 'Tell me what you like, and I will tell you the kind of man you are.'

The second consideration is this. The words 'good' and 'bad' have so many connotations in their various moral and non-moral usages that it is difficult to find any residuum in them that is universal. Yet I think it would be impossible to find any reasonable man who would frankly maintain that, in any walk of life, it is just as well to like the bad as to like the good. Unless you maintain this, you are surely granting that not only in art that is great, but also in its lesser embodiments—in its humorous drawings, its light verse, its two-steps—there is a certain moral obligation on us to discern what is good and demand a standard of clean intention and competent craftsmanship.

Throughout these lectures I have been beset by the difficulty of balancing and harmonizing the aims I set before myself at the start. You may complain I have given you too few facts, for I have tried not to give you too many. You may also complain I have not laid bare many principles, for I have tried to lead you to grasp them by your own intelligence. I have aimed at opening your minds and not at filling them, at whetting your curiosity, not at satisfying it. For I believe that in music, as in everything, the only knowledge worth having is what we find out for ourselves, and that though a guide may help us on our journey and save us from many pitfalls, yet the best guide is the one who can teach us to do without him.

It is a common practice for an author to give, at the end of his book, an inventory of the authorities on which he has drawn for his doctrines. It is the equally common practice of his readers to omit that particular chapter, since they find, from previous experience, that it serves to advertise the wide reading of the writer rather than to help the student to continue his research.

Nevertheless, I should like to make an attempt at telling musical students about the books and essays which I think they ought to read if they wish to grip more than the bare outlines of the subjects on which I have spoken; and I have grouped them, for the reader's ease, under the headings of the various lectures. No one will read them all, even though the lists are small and very far from exhaustive, but I should advise any student who is in earnest to read at least one in each group.

BIBLIOGRAPHY

Lecture I. The Raw Material of Music

Elementary:

A. Wood: *The Physical Basis of Music* (Cambridge University Press).

Harris: *Handbook of Acoustics* (Curwen).

Sedley Taylor: *Sound and Music* (Macmillan).

Kelvin: '*The Six Gateways of Knowledge*' (in Sir W. Thomson's *Popular Lectures and Addresses*, vol. i, Macmillan).

Bragg: *The World of Sound* (Bell).

Buck: *Acoustics for Musicians* (Oxford University Press).

Pole: *The Philosophy of Music* (Kegan Paul).

Advanced:

Helmholtz: *Sensations of Tone* (Longmans).

Barton: *Text-book on Sound* (Macmillan).

Lecture II. The Origin of Music

Spencer: Essay on *The Origin and Function of Music* (Williams & Norgate).

C. Engel: *An Introduction to The Study of National Music* (Longmans).

C. Engel: *The Music of the most Ancient Nations* (Murray).

Parry: *The Art of Music* (Kegan Paul).

E. Newman: '*Herbert Spencer and the Origin of Music*' (in *Musical Studies*, Lane).

Wagner: *Art and Revolution* (in prose works, vol. i, Kegan Paul).

Abdy Williams: *The Aristoxenian Theory of Musical Rhythm* (Cambridge University Press).

C. S. Myers: '*A Study of Rhythm in Primitive Music*' (*British Journal of Psychology*, vol. xx, pt. iv).

Jane Harrison: *Ancient Art and Ritual* (Williams & Norgate).

Lecture III. The Nature of Beauty

Vernon Lee: *The Beautiful* (Cambridge University Press).

Knight: *The Philosophy of the Beautiful* (Murray).

Sully: '*Sensation and Intuition*,' Essay 13, *On the possibility of a Science of Aesthetics* (King).

Lessing: *Laocoön* (Bell).

Hegel: *Philosophy of Fine Art* (introduction) (Bell).

Grant Allen: '*The Differentia of Aesthetics*' (chap. 3 in *Physiological Aesthetics*; King).

LECTURE IV. CRITICISM

Calvocoressi : *Musical Criticism* (Oxford University Press).
Lamborn : *Rudiments of Criticism* (Oxford University Press).
J. A. Symonds : ' *On some Principles of Criticism* ' (in *Essays, Speculative and Suggestive* ; Murray).
Hadow : *Studies in Modern Music*, vol. i (Seeley).

LECTURE V. APPRECIATION

Hadow : *Studies in Modern Music*, vol. ii (Seeley).
Lloyd Morgan : *Psychology for Teachers*, chap. ix (Arnold).
Coventry Patmore : ' *Religio Poetae*,' chapters on *Emotional Art* and *Distinction* (Bell).

LECTURE VI. FALLACIES

G. B. Shaw : *The Sanity of Art* (Constable).
W. Archer : *Art and the Commonwealth* (Watts).
Grant Allen : ' *Postprandial Philosophy*,' essay, *Anent Art-production* (Chatto & Windus).
G. K. Chesterton : ' *A Defence of Nonsense* ' and ' *A Defence of Ugly Things* ' (both in *The Defendant*, Dent).
G. K. Chesterton : ' *The Mystagogue* ' (in *A Miscellany of Men* ; Methuen).

LECTURE VII. THE PLACE OF MUSIC AMONGST THE ARTS

Hadow : *Studies in Modern Music*, vol. i (Seeley).
J. A. Symonds : ' *The provinces of the several Arts* ' and ' *Is Music the type or measure of all Art?* ' both in *Essays, Speculative and Suggestive* (Murray).
Sully : ' *Sensation and Intuition*,' Essay 11, on *The representation of Character in Art* (King).
Schopenhauer : *The World as Will and Idea*, book iii (Kegan Paul).
Grant Allen : ' *Physiological Aesthetics*,' chap. x on *The Imitative Arts* (King).

LECTURES VIII AND IX. MELODY AND FORM

Hadow : *Sonata Form* (Novello).
Sully : ' *Sensation and Intuition*,' Essay 8, on *Aspects of Beauty in Musical Form* (King).
R. A. M. Stevenson : ' *Velasquez*,' chap. iv, on *The Dignity of Technique* (Bell).
J. B. McEwen : ' *Foundations of Musical Aesthetics*,' chap. vii, on *The Principles of Rhythmic Balance* (Kegan Paul).
Parry : *Style in Musical Art*, especially chaps. vi, xii, and xiii (Macmillan).
Hadow : *Studies in Modern Music*, vol. ii (Seeley).

LECTURE X. MUSIC AND PSYCHOLOGY

Mrs. J. S. Curwen : *Psychology applied to Music Teaching* (Curwen).
James : *Talks to Teachers on Psychology* (Longmans).
McDougall : *Social Psychology* (Methuen).
J. B. McEwen : *The Thought in Music* (Macmillan).
Wallace : *The Threshold of Music* (Macmillan).
Wallace : *The Musical Faculty* (Macmillan).
Sully : '*Sensation and Intuition*,' Essay 10, on *The Aesthetic Aspects of Character* (King).
Gurney : *The Power of Sound* (Murray).